THE PROPERTY FINANCE SOURCEBOOK 2002

Compiled and edited by **Richard von Götzen**

Estates gazette

A member of Reed Business Information

First published 1994
Second edition published 1999
Third edition published 2000
This edition published 2002

ISBN 0 7282 0384 7
Printed and bound by Cromwell Press, Trowbridge, Wiltshire

Contents

Introduction

by Richard von Götzen

Another year has passed and it only remains for me to thank all the many principal lenders for their continued support and assistance, without which it would be impossible to produce the Property Finance Sourcebook.

It is only as a result of the ongoing help and co-operation of these lenders that the Property Finance Sourcebook has been able to establish itself as the prime reference for the funding of commercial and residential investment properties, as well as for development finance in the UK. It is still very much our goal to build on this. In order to help us do so, we very much welcome any feedback from the users of the directory, for whom after all it has been produced. Comments and suggestions should be addressed to the editor.

How to use the Sourcebook

Our objective remains to provide information on all known lenders in the UK commercial property industry, together with as detailed a loan criteria as possible. Readers should, however, continue to view and use the Sourcebook primarily as a broad guide because lenders will always evaluate propositions on a case by case basis.

Borrowers should, in the first instance, always telephone the named contact at the lending institution and provide outlined particulars of the property to be financed. Only once this outline has been met with a positive response will it usually be necessary to send a complete package of information to then enable the lender to make a written conditional proposal or offer. This offer is always subject to a satisfactory independent valuation being obtained, usually at the expense of the borrower, and is further subject to contract.

A good, clear and concise presentation of the proposal requiring funding is vital, especially as most lenders receive a large number of competing propositions each day. The feedback received from lenders continues to underline this aspect which still seems the most neglected by borrowers. It is the best presented and easiest to understand proposals that are most likely to receive the earliest and most favourable consideration. That said, written proposals should be as brief as possible and to the point.

Initially, the most important information that the lending institutions will need to know and will require verification for are:

1. The status and background of the borrower. In today's market there is no question that the track record of the borrower remains vital.
2. Brief details and a description of the property or project being proposed.
3. The extent of loan security afforded by the covenant, together with the length and the terms of such lease where applicable.

4. The security and revenue cash flow of the property or project, the potential for upside return and sensitivity to risk.

The mainstream lenders still remain driven by covenant strength and therefore as much relevant information as possible (the covenant's standing etc.) should be included.

In order to secure a written quotation or offer of financing from a lending institution, the following should be sent with a proposal (not in any order of importance).

The Borrower

1. Audited accounts for the last three years and a statement of assets and liabilities. In the absence of audited accounts, certified or management accounts may in some cases be acceptable.
2. A Curriculum Vitae for all the principals of the borrowing company or for the borrower where appropriate.
3. A business plan if relevant.

The Property

4. Full details of the tenants, tenancies, rental income and the latest annual report and accounts for the tenants where available.
5. Copy of a recent valuation if available.
6. Photograph of the property.
7. The amount of loan requested, period for which required and the type of loan, i.e. fixed, bullet or variable interest payments.

Developments

8. A full business plan. (Absolutely vital.)
9. Complete details of the proposed development to include specifications, proposed contractor, architect and developer, together with cash flows, projections and details of any pre-lets or pre-sales.
10. A market analysis of occupier demand and supply for the type of property proposed in the geographical locality.

All in all, the increased number of lenders, the expansion of the sectors and the improved criteria on offer once again afford the borrower the best and most competitive opportunity for funding for many years.

We very much hope this Sourcebook eases the search.

Richard von Götzen
Editor

April 2002

Glossary of terms used

Arrangement fee	A fee charged by the lender to cover its administrative costs. Generally the more complicated the loan, the higher the fee.
Amortization	Capital repayment of the loan. Usually a percentage per annum on top of the loan.
Balloon payment	The largest repayment of a loan usually repaid by instalments. Normally paid at the beginning and/or end of a loan.
Base rate	The basic rate of interest.
Basis point	One hundredth of one percent.
Bridging finance	An interim loan enabling the borrower to later refinance the proposal.
Bricks and mortar	The value of the standing asset vacant.
Bullet	Lump sum repayment of the loan at the end of the loan term.
Building society cost of funds	The cost at which the building societies borrow money.
Cap	An arrangement ensuring an upper limit on the interest rate payable on a variable or floating rate loan. The cap comes into play if interest rates move above the level of the cap.
Carried interest	A profit share over and above the return received by a lender or principal once their loan has been repaid.
Collar	Same as a cap only that in addition to an upper limit there is also a lower limit, in which case the borrower continues to pay at collar level – even if interest rates fall.
Cost of funds	The cost of borrowing in the money market.
Covenant	The tenant of the property.
Debt finance	Usually a first charge as mortgage.
Equity finance	Participation by the lender or investor in the project or property.
FHBR	Finance House Base Rate.
Fixed	Rate of interest is fixed at an amount for a specified period.
Floating rate	Interest rate which fluctuates to changes in Libor.
Interest only	A loan without amortization where interest only is payable.
Libor	London Interbank offered rate. The rate at which banks lend to one another.
LTV	Loan to Value. The amount of loan as a percentage of the value.

Margin The percentage over whatever benchmark at which the lender is prepared to lend money.

Mezzanine finance A loan over and above the LTV. Because of the risk factor involved in such loans they tend to be expensive.

Structured finance Bespoke financing.

Pre-let A binding commitment from an occupier before construction of a building is completed to enter into a lease on specific terms for the building.

Swap The cost of swapping funds with another lender in the international market. Can be applied to the rate, type and currency etc.

LENDER INDICES

BY SPECIALISMS

The following lenders have indicated they will consider loans in specific markets

AGRICULTURE

AGRICULTURAL MORTGAGE CORPORATION PLC
BANK OF SCOTLAND (CENTREBANK)
BANK OF WALES
BARCLAYS BANK PLC
LLOYDS TSB
MIDLAND BANK
NATIONAL COUNTIES BUILDING SOCIETY
NATIONAL WESTMINSTER BANK PLC
NORTHERN BANK LTD
ROYAL BANK OF SCOTLAND
SCOTTISH AGRICULTURAL SECURITIES CORPORATION PLC
YORKSHIRE BANK PLC

PROVIDERS OF BRIDGING LOANS

AAREAL BANK
HENRY ANSBACHER & CO
ARBUTHNOT LATHAM & CO
BHF BANK
BALTIC PROPERTY FINANCE PLC
BANK JULIUS BAER & CO
BANK LEUMI (UK) PLC
BANK OF TOKYO - MITSUBISHI
BANK OF WALES
BANKERS TRUST COMPANY
BARCLAYS BANK PLC
BAYERISCHE VEREINSBANK AG
BRITISH ARAB COMMERCIAL BANK LTD
CHARTERHOUSE PROPERTY FINANCE LTD
CHASE MANHATTAN, J P MORGAN
CITY GROUP
CLOSE BROTHERS LTD
COMMERCIAL ACCEPTANCES
DEPFA BANK AG
DEUTSCHE BANK AG
ERSTE BANK
G E CAPITAL REAL ESTATE
GOLDMAN SACHS REAL ESTATE PRINCIPAL INVESTMENT
GRANVILLE BANK LTD
HSBC BANK PLC
HAMPSHIRE TRUST PLC
HERITABLE BANK LTD
HOLBORN SECURITIES PLC
HYPOVEREINSBANK REAL ESTATE CAPITAL
INTERMEDIATE CAPITAL GROUP PLC
INVESTEC BANK (UK) LTD

MERRILL LYNCH INTERNATIONAL LTD
J P MORGAN & CO
MORGAN GUARANTY TRUST CO (J P MORGAN)
NATIONAL WESTMINSTER BANK PLC
NOMURA BANK INTERNATIONAL
NORTHERN BANK LTD
PROPERTY MEZZANINE PARTNERS
REGENTSMEAD LTD
SINGER & FRIEDLANDER
UNION BANK OF SWITZERLAND
UNITED BANK OF KUWAIT PLC
UNITED TRUST BANK LTD
WESTDEUTSCHE IMMOBILIEN BANK
WINTRUST SECURITIES LTD

EQUITY FINANCE
AAREAL BANK
HENRY ANSBACHER & CO
BHF BANK AG
BALTIC PROPERTY FINANCE PLC
BANK LEUMI (UK) PLC
BANKERS TRUST COMPANY
CHARTERHOUSE PROPERTY FINANCE
CHASE MANHATTAN, J P MORGAN
CITY GROUP
CLOSE BROTHERS LTD
DEUTSCHE BANK AG
G E CAPITAL REAL ESTATE
GOLDMAN SACHS REAL ESTATE PRINCIPAL INVESTMENT
GRANVILLE BANK LTD
HSBC INVESTMENT BANK PLC
HOLBORN SECURITIES PLC
INTERMEDIATE CAPITAL GROUP PLC
J P MORGAN & CO
MORGAN STANLEY DEAN WITTER
PROPERTY MEZZANINE PARTNERS

DEVELOPMENT PROPERTIES
ALLIANCE & LEICESTER (GIRO BANK)
ALLIED IRISH BANK
ANGLO IRISH BANK CORPORATION PLC
HENRY ANSBACHER & CO
ARBUTHNOT LATHAM & CO
BHF BANK AG
BALTIC PROPERTY FINANCE PLC
BANK LEUMI (UK) PLC
BANK OF SCOTLAND (CENTREBANK)
BANK OF TOKYO – MITSUBISHI
BANK OF WALES PLC
BARCLAYS BANK PLC
BAYERISCHE VEREINSBANK AG

BROWN SHIPLEY & CO
CHARTERHOUSE PROPERTY FINANCE LTD
CHASE MANHATTAN, J P MORGAN
CHELSEA BUILDING SOCIETY
CITY GROUP
CLOSE BROTHERS LTD
CLYDESDALE BANK
COMMERCIAL ACCEPTANCES
CREDIT AGRICOLE INDOSUEZ
CREDIT LYONNAIS
DEPFA BANK AG
DEUTSCHE BANK AG
DEUTSCHE HYP AG
DEUTSCHE HYPO
DUNBAR GROUP PLC
DUNFERMLINE BUILDING SOCIETY
ERSTE BANK
EUROHYPO
FURNESS BUILDING SOCIETY
G E CAPITAL REAL ESTATE
GIRO BANK (SEE ALLIANCE & LEICESTER)
GOLDMAN SACHS REAL ESTATE PRINCIPAL INVESTMENT
GRANVILLE BANK LTD
HSBC INVESTMENT BANK PLC
HAMPSHIRE TRUST PLC
HERITABLE BANK LTD
JULIAN HODGE BANK LTD
HOLBORN SECURITIES PLC
HYPOVEREINSBANK REAL ESTATE CAPITAL
INTERMEDIATE CAPITAL GROUP PLC
INVESTEC BANK (UK) LTD
KBC BANK NV
LANDESBANK HESSEN-THÜRINGEN (HELABA)
LEOPOLD JOSEPH & SONS LTD
LLOYDS TSB
W M MANN & CO (INVESTMENTS) LTD
MERRILL LYNCH INTERNATIONAL LTD
MIDLAND BANK
J P MORGAN & CO
MORGAN STANLEY DEAN WITTER
NATIONAL WESTMINSTER BANK PLC
NEWBURY BUILDING SOCIETY
NORDEA
NORTHERN BANK LTD
P L T LTD
PRINCIPALITY BUILDING SOCIETY
REGENTSMEAD LTD
REPUBLIC NATIONAL BANK OF NEW YORK
RIGGS BANK EUROPE LTD
N M ROTHSCHILD & SONS
THE ROYAL BANK OF SCOTLAND PLC

SAFFRON WALDEN HERTS & ESSEX BUILDING SOCIETY
SANWA BANK
SINGER & FRIEDLANDER
SOCIÉTÉ GÉNÉRALE
SUMITOMO BANK
SUN LIFE OF CANADA GROUP OF COMPANIES
UCB GROUP
ULSTER BANK LTD
UNION BANK OF SWITZERLAND
UNITED ASSET FINANCE LTD
UNITED BANK OF KUWAIT PLC
UNITED TRUST BANK LTD
VERNON BUILDING SOCIETY
WESTDEUTSCHE IMMOBILIEN BANK
THE WESTHYP WESTFÄLISCHE HYPOTHEKENBANK AG
WINTRUST SECURITIES LTD
YORKSHIRE BANK PLC

HEALTHCARE
ABBEY NATIONAL PLC
ALLCHURCHES MORTGAGE COMPANY
ALLIANCE & LEICESTER (GIRO BANK)
ALLIED DUNBAR PROVIDENT
ALLIED IRISH BANK
ANGLO IRISH BANK CORPORATION
ARBUTHNOT LATHAM & CO
BANK LEUMI (UK) PLC
BANK OF SCOTLAND (CENTREBANK)
BARNSLEY BUILDING SOCIETY
BIRMINGHAM MIDSHIRES
BRITISH ARAB COMMERCIAL BANK LTD
CHARTERHOUSE PROPERTY FINANCE LTD
CHASE MANHATTAN, J P MORGAN
CITIBANK INTERNATIONAL PLC
CITY GROUP
CLOSE BROTHERS LTD
CREDIT AGRICOLE INDOSUEZ
DEUTSCHE BANK AG
EAGLE STAR MORTGAGES LTD
ERSTE BANK
HSBC BANK PLC
HAMPSHIRE TRUST PLC
LLOYDS TSB
MANCHESTER BUILDING SOCIETY
MERRILL LYNCH INTERNATIONAL LTD
MIDLAND BANK
J P MORGAN & CO
NATIONAL WESTMINSTER BANK PLC
NEWBURY BUILDING SOCIETY
NORTHERN BANK LTD
NORTHERN ROCK PLC

NORWICH & PETERBOROUGH BUILDING SOCIETY
NORWICH UNION PLC
PRINCIPALITY BUILDING SOCIETY
N M ROTHSCHILD & SONS
THE ROYAL BANK OF SCOTLAND PLC
UCB GROUP PLC
UNITED BANK OF KUWAIT PLC
WEST BROMWICH BUILDING SOCIETY
YORKSHIRE BANK PLC

HOTELS AND LEISURE
AAREAL BANK
ABBEY NATIONAL PLC
ALLCHURCHES MORTGAGE COMPANY
ALLIED IRISH BANK
ANGLO IRISH BANK CORPORATION PLC
ARBUTHNOT LATHAM & CO
BHF BANK AG
BANK JULIUS BAER & CO
BANK LEUMI (UK) PLC
BANK OF SCOTLAND (CENTREBANK)
BANK OF WALES PLC
BARCLAYS BANK PLC
BARNSLEY BUILDING SOCIETY
BATH BUILDING SOCIETY
BIRMINGHAM MIDSHIRES
BRITISH ARAB COMMERCIAL BANK LTD
CANADA LIFE LTD
CHARTERHOUSE PROPERTY FINANCE LTD
CHASE MANHATTAN, J P MORGAN
CHESHIRE BUILDING SOCIETY
CITY GROUP
CLYDESDALE BANK
CO-OPERATIVE BANK
DARLINGTON BUILDING SOCIETY
DEUTSCHE BANK AG
DEUTSCHE HYP AG
DEUTSCHE HYPO
ERSTE BANK
FIRST NATIONAL BANK
GOLDMAN SACHS REAL ESTATE PRINCIPAL INVESTMENT
HSBC BANK PLC
HAMPSHIRE TRUST PLC
HOLBORN SECURITIES PLC
INTERMEDIATE CAPITAL GROUP PLC
INVESTEC BANK (UK) LTD
LAMBETH BUILDING SOCIETY
LLOYDS TSB
MANCHESTER BUILDING SOCIETY
MANSFIELD BUILDING SOCIETY
MARSDEN BUILDING SOCIETY

MERRILL LYNCH INTERNATIONAL LTD
MIDLAND BANK
J P MORGAN & CO
NATIONAL WESTMINSTER BANK PLC
NEWBURY BUILDING SOCIETY
NORDEA
NORTHERN BANK LTD
NORTHERN ROCK PLC
NORWICH & PETERBOROUGH BUILDING SOCIETY
NORWICH UNION PLC
PRINCIPALITY BUILDING SOCIETY
N M ROTHSCHILD & SONS LTD
THE ROYAL BANK OF SCOTLAND PLC
SANWA BANK
UNIVERSAL BUILDING SOCIETY
VERNON BUILDING SOCIETY
WESTDEUTSCHE IMMOBILIEN BANK
YORKSHIRE BANK PLC

INVESTMENT PROPERTIES
AAREAL BANK
ABBEY NATIONAL PLC
ALLCHURCHES MORTGAGE COMPANY
ALLIANCE & LEICESTER (GIRO BANK)
ALLIED DUNBAR PROVIDENT
ALLIED IRISH BANK
ANGLO IRISH BANK CORPORATION PLC
HENRY ANSBACHER & CO
ARBUTHNOT LATHAM & CO
BHF BANK AG
BANK JULIUS BAER & CO
BANK LEUMI (UK) PLC
THE BANK OF EAST ASIA
BANK OF SCOTLAND (CENTREBANK)
BANK OF TOKYO – MITSUBISHI
BANK OF WALES PLC
BANKERS TRUST COMPANY
BARCLAYS BANK PLC
BARNSLEY BUILDING SOCIETY
BATH BUILDING SOCIETY
BAYERISCHE VEREINSBANK AG
BIRMINGHAM MIDSHIRES
BRADFORD & BINGLEY PLC
BRISTOL & WEST PLC
BRITISH ARAB COMMERCIAL BANK LTD
THE BRITISH LINEN BANK LTD
BROWN SHIPLEY & CO
CAMBRIDGE BUILDING SOCIETY
CANADA LIFE LTD
CHARTERHOUSE PROPERTY FINANCE LTD
CHASE MANHATTAN, J P MORGAN

CHESHIRE BUILDING SOCIETY
CITIBANK INTERNATIONAL PLC
CITY GROUP
CLOSE BROTHERS LTD
CLYDESDALE BANK
COMMERCIAL ACCEPTANCES
CO-OPERATIVE BANK
COVENTRY BUILDING SOCIETY
CREDIT AGRICOLE INDOSUEZ
CREDIT LYONNAIS
DARLINGTON BUILDING SOCIETY
DEPFA BANK AG
DERBYSHIRE BUILDING SOCIETY
DEUTSCHE BANK AG
DEUTSCHE GENOSSENSCHAFTS HYPOTHEKENBANK
DEUTSCHE HYP AG
DEUTSCHE HYPO
DUNBAR GROUP PLC
DUNFERMLINE BUILDING SOCIETY
EAGLE STAR MORTGAGES LTD
ERSTE BANK
EUROHYPO
FIRST NATIONAL BANK
FIRST NATIONAL BUILDING SOCIETY
FURNESS BUILDING SOCIETY
G E CAPITAL REAL ESTATE
GOLDMAN SACHS REAL ESTATE PRINCIPAL INVESTMENT
GRANVILLE BANK LTD
HSBC BANK PLC
HAMBURGISCHE LANDESBANK
HAMPSHIRE TRUST PLC
HINCKLEY & RUGBY BUILDING SOCIETY
JULIAN HODGE BANK LTD
HOLBORN SECURITIES PLC
HYPOVEREINSBANK REAL ESTATE CAPITAL
INVESTEC BANK (UK) LTD
KBC BANK NV
KENT RELIANCE BUILDING SOCIETY
LAMBETH BUILDING SOCIETY
LANDESBANK HESSEN-THÜRINGEN (HELABA)
LEEK UNITED BUILDING SOCIETY
LEGAL & GENERAL BANK
LEOPOLD JOSEPH & SONS LTD
LIVERPOOL & VICTORIA
LLOYDS TSB
MANCHESTER BUILDING SOCIETY
W M MANN & CO (INVESTMENTS) LTD
MANSFIELD BUILDING SOCIETY
MARSDEN BUILDING SOCIETY
MERCANTILE BUILDING SOCIETY
MERRILL LYNCH INTERNATIONAL LTD

MIDLAND BANK
J P MORGAN & CO
MORGAN STANLEY DEAN WITTER
NATIONAL COUNTIES BUILDING SOCIETY
NATIONAL WESTMINSTER BANK PLC
NATIONWIDE BUILDING SOCIETY
NEWBURY BUILDING SOCIETY
NEWCASTLE BUILDING SOCIETY
NOMURA BANK INTERNATIONAL
NORDEA
NORTHERN BANK LTD
NORTHERN ROCK PLC
NORWICH & PETERBOROUGH BUILDING SOCIETY
NORWICH UNION PLC
PORTMAN BUILDING SOCIETY
PRINCIPALITY BUILDING SOCIETY
PRUDENTIAL PORTFOLIO MANAGERS LTD
REGENTSMEAD LTD
REPUBLIC NATIONAL BANK OF NEW YORK
RIGGS BANK EUROPE LTD
N M ROTHSCHILD & SONS
THE ROYAL BANK OF SCOTLAND PLC
SAFFRON WALDEN HERTS & ESSEX BUILDING SOCIETY
SANWA BANK
SINGER & FRIEDLANDER
SOCIÉTÉ GÉNÉRALE
SÜDDEUTSCHE BODENCREDIT & HYPOTHEKENBANK AG
SUMITOMO BANK
SUN BANK PLC
SUN LIFE OF CANADA GROUP OF COMPANIES
SVENSKA HANDELSBANKEN
UBS WARBURG
ULSTER BANK LTD
UNION BANK OF SWITZERLAND
UNITED ASSET FINANCE LTD
UNITED BANK OF KUWAIT PLC
UNIVERSAL BUILDING SOCIETY
VERNON BUILDING SOCIETY
WEST BROMWICH BUILDING SOCIETY
WESTDEUTSCHE IMMOBILIEN BANK
THE WESTHYP WESTFÄLISCHE HYPOTHEKENBANK AG
WINTRUST SECURITIES LTD
WÜRTTEMBERGER HYPO
YORKSHIRE BANK PLC

PROVIDERS OF MEZZANINE FINANCE

HENRY ANSBACHER & CO
BHF BANK AG
BALTIC PROPERTY FINANCE PLC
BANK LEUMI (UK) PLC
BANKERS TRUST COMPANY

BANK JULIUS BAER & CO
BANK OF TOKYO - MITSUBISHI
BAYERISCHE VEREINSBANK AG
BRITISH ARAB COMMERCIAL BANK LTD
CHARTERHOUSE PROPERTY FINANCE LTD
CHASE MANHATTAN, J P MORGAN
CITY GROUP
CLOSE BROTHERS LTD
COMMERCIAL ACCEPTANCES
DEPFA BANK AG
G E CAPITAL REAL ESTATE
GOLDMAN SACHS REAL ESTATE PRINCIPAL INVESTMENT
GRANVILLE BANK LTD
HSBC BANK PLC
HYPOVEREINSBANK REAL ESTATE CAPITAL
INTERMEDIATE CAPITAL GROUP PLC
INVESTEC BANK (UK) LTD
MANCHESTER BUILDING SOCIETY
MERRILL LYNCH INTERNATIONAL LTD
J P MORGAN & CO
MORGAN GUARANTY TRUST CO (J P MORGAN)
NOMURA BANK INTERNATIONAL
PROPERTY MEZZANINE PARTNERS
SINGER & FRIEDLANDER
UNION BANK OF SWITZERLAND
UNITED BANK OF KUWAIT PLC
WESTDEUTSCHE IMMOBILIEN BANK
WINTRUST SECURITIES LTD

SPECULATIVE OR PART PRE-LET DEVELOPMENT

ALLIANCE & LEICESTER (GIRO BANK)
ALLIED IRISH BANK
ARBUTHNOT LATHAM & CO
BHF BANK AG
BALTIC PROPERTY FINANCE PLC
BANK LEUMI (UK) PLC
CHASE MANHATTAN, J P MORGAN
ERSTE BANK
GRANVILLE BANK LTD
HAMPSHIRE TRUST PLC
KBC BANK NV
LANDESBANK HESSEN-THÜRINGEN (HELABA)
REGENTSMEAD LTD
UNITED BANK OF KUWAIT PLC

REGIONAL LENDERS

THE BANK OF EAST ASIA	LONDON
BATH BUILDING SOCIETY	30-MILE RADIUS OF BATH
CAMBRIDGE BUILDING SOCIETY	50-MILE RADIUS OF CAMBRIDGE
COVENTRY BUILDING SOCIETY	50-MILE RADIUS OF COVENTRY

DARLINGTON BUILDING SOCIETY	S. DURHAM & N. YORKSHIRE
DUNFERMLINE BUILDING SOCIETY	N. ENGLAND & SCOTLAND
FIRST NATIONAL BUILDING SOCIETY	IRISH REPUBLIC
FURNESS BUILDING SOCIETY	100-MILE RADIUS OF BARROW-IN-FURNESS
HINCKLEY & RUGBY BUILDING SOCIETY	EAST MIDLANDS
LEEK UNITED BUILDING SOCIETY	60-MILE RADIUS OF LEEK
MANCHESTER BUILDING SOCIETY	50-MILE RADIUS OF MANCHESTER
NORTHERN BANK LTD	N. IRELAND ONLY
W M MANN & CO (INVESTMENTS) LTD	SCOTLAND ONLY
MARSDEN BUILDING SOCIETY	100-MILE RADIUS OF MARSDEN
NEWBURY BUILDING SOCIETY	60-MILE RADIUS OF NEWBURY
PORTMAN BUILDING SOCIETY	CENTRAL LONDON ONLY
PRINCIPALITY BUILDING SOCIETY	WALES ONLY
ULSTER BANK LTD	N. IRELAND AND REPUBLIC OF IRELAND ONLY

RESIDENTIAL DEVELOPMENT

ANGLO IRISH BANK CORPORATION PLC
BHF BANK AG
BALTIC PROPERTY FINANCE PLC
BARCLAYS BANK PLC
CITY GROUP
COMMERCIAL ACCEPTANCES
DUNBAR GROUP PLC
ERSTE BANK
FURNESS BUILDING SOCIETY
GRANVILLE BANK LTD
HAMPSHIRE TRUST PLC
HERITABLE BANK LTD
JULIAN HODGE BANK LTD
P L T LTD
PRINCIPALITY BUILDING SOCIETY
REGENTSMEAD LTD
RIGGS BANK EUROPE LTD
SAINSBURY'S BANK
WINTRUST SECURITIES LTD

OWNER OCCUPIER

ABBEY NATIONAL PLC
AGRICULTURAL MORTGAGE CORPORATION PLC
ALLCHURCHES MORTGAGE COMPANY
ALLIANCE & LEICESTER (GIRO BANK)
ALLIED DUNBAR PROVIDENT
ALLIED IRISH BANK
ARBUTHNOT LATHAM & CO
BHF BANK AG
BALTIC PROPERTY FINANCE PLC

BANK JULIUS BAER & CO
THE BANK OF EAST ASIA
BANK OF SCOTLAND (CENTREBANK)
BANK OF TOKYO – MITSUBISHI
BANK OF WALES PLC
BANKERS TRUST COMPANY
BARCLAYS BANK PLC
BARNSLEY BUILDING SOCIETY
BATH BUILDING SOCIETY
BAYERISCHE VEREINSBANK AG
BIRMINGHAM MIDSHIRES
BRADFORD & BINGLEY PLC
BRITISH LINEN BANK LTD
BROWN SHIPLEY & CO
CAMBRIDGE BUILDING SOCIETY
CAPITAL HOME LOANS LTD
CHASE MANHATTAN, J P MORGAN
CHELSEA BUILDING SOCIETY
CHESHIRE BUILDING SOCIETY
CITIBANK INTERNATIONAL PLC
CITY GROUP
CLYDESDALE BANK
COMMERCIAL ACCEPTANCES
CO-OPERATIVE BANK
CREDIT AGRICOLE INDOSUEZ
CREDIT LYONNAIS
DARLINGTON BUILDING SOCIETY
DEPFA BANK AG
DERBYSHIRE BUILDING SOCIETY
DEUTSCHE BANK AG
DEUTSCHE HYP AG
DEUTSCHE HYPO
DUNFERMLINE BUILDING SOCIETY
EUROHYPO
FIRST NATIONAL BANK
FIRST NATIONAL BUILDING SOCIETY
FURNESS BUILDING SOCIETY
G E CAPITAL REAL ESTATE
GOLDMAN SACHS REAL ESTATE PRINCIPAL INVESTMENT
GRANVILLE BANK LTD
HSBC BANK PLC
HAMBURGISCHE LANDESBANK
HAMPSHIRE TRUST PLC
HINCKLEY & RUGBY BUILDING SOCIETY
JULIAN HODGE BANK LTD
HOLBORN SECURITIES PLC
HYPOVEREINSBANK REAL ESTATE CAPITAL
INVESTEC BANK (UK) LTD
KENT RELIANCE BUILDING SOCIETY
LAMBETH BUILDING SOCIETY
LANDESBANK HESSEN-THÜRINGEN (HELABA)

LEEK UNITED BUILDING SOCIETY
LEGAL & GENERAL BANK
LEOPOLD JOSEPH & SONS LTD
LLOYDS TSB
MANCHESTER BUILDING SOCIETY
W M MANN & CO (INVESTMENTS) LTD
MANSFIELD BUILDING SOCIETY
MARSDEN BUILDING SOCIETY
MERCANTILE BUILDING SOCIETY
MIDLAND BANK
J P MORGAN & CO
NATIONAL COUNTIES BUILDING SOCIETY
NATIONAL WESTMINSTER BANK PLC
NATIONWIDE BUILDING SOCIETY
NEWBURY BUILDING SOCIETY
NEWCASTLE BUILDING SOCIETY
NOMURA BANK INTERNATIONAL
NORDEA
NORTHERN BANK LTD
NORTHERN ROCK PLC
NORWICH & PETERBOROUGH BUILDING SOCIETY
PORTMAN BUILDING SOCIETY
PRINCIPALITY BUILDING SOCIETY
PRUDENTIAL PORTFOLIO MANAGERS LTD
REGENTSMEAD LTD
RHEINISCHE HYPOTHEKENBANK AG
N M ROTHSCHILD & SONS
THE ROYAL BANK OF SCOTLAND PLC
SAFFRON WALDEN HERTS & ESSEX BUILDING SOCIETY
SANWA BANK
SCOTTISH AGRICULTURAL SECURITIES CORPORATION PLC
SUN LIFE OF CANADA GROUP OF COMPANIES
SVENSKA HANDELSBANKEN
UBS WARBURG
UCB GROUP PLC
ULSTER BANK LTD
UNION BANK OF SWITZERLAND
UNITED ASSET FINANCE LTD
UNIVERSAL BUILDING SOCIETY
VERNON BUILDING SOCIETY
WEST BROMWICH BUILDING SOCIETY
WESTDEUTSCHE IMMOBILIEN BANK
THE WESTHYP WESTFÄLISCHE HYPOTHEKENBANK AG
WÜRTTEMBERGER HYPO
YORKSHIRE BANK PLC

RESIDENTIAL INVESTMENTS
ALLCHURCHES MORTGAGE COMPANY
ANGLO IRISH BANK CORPORATION PLC
BHF BANK AG
BANK JULIUS BAER & CO

BANK LEUMI (UK) PLC
THE BANK OF EAST ASIA
BANK OF WALES PLC
BARCLAYS BANK PLC
BIRMINGHAM MIDSHIRES
BRISTOL & WEST PLC
THE BRITISH LINEN BANK LTD
BROWN SHIPLEY & CO
CAMBRIDGE BUILDING SOCIETY
CAPITAL HOME LOANS LTD
CHARTERHOUSE PROPERTY FINANCE LTD
CHELSEA BUILDING SOCIETY
CHESHIRE BUILDING SOCIETY
CITIBANK INTERNATIONAL PLC
CLOSE BROTHERS LTD
CLYDESDALE BANK
COMMERCIAL ACCEPTANCES
COVENTRY BUILDING SOCIETY
DARLINGTON BUILDING SOCIETY
DEPFA BANK AG
DERBYSHIRE BUILDING SOCIETY
DEUTSCHE HYP AG
DEUTSCHE HYPO
DUNBAR GROUP PLC
DUNFERMLINE BUILDING SOCIETY
FIRST NATIONAL BANK
FIRST NATIONAL BUILDING SOCIETY
FURNESS BUILDING SOCIETY
GRANVILLE BANK LTD
HSBC BANK PLC
HAMBURGISCHE LANDESBANK
HAMPSHIRE TRUST PLC
HINCKLEY & RUGBY BUILDING SOCIETY
HOLBORN SECURITIES PLC
HYPOVEREINSBANK REAL ESTATE CAPITAL
KENT RELIANCE BUILDING SOCIETY
LAMBETH BUILDING SOCIETY
LANDESBANK HESSEN-THÜRINGEN (HELABA)
LEEK UNITED BUILDING SOCIETY
LEOPOLD JOSEPH & SONS LTD
LLOYDS TSB
MANCHESTER BUILDING SOCIETY
W M MANN & CO (INVESTMENTS) LTD
MANSFIELD BUILDING SOCIETY
MARSDEN BUILDING SOCIETY
MERCANTILE BUILDING SOCIETY
MIDLAND BANK
J P MORGAN & CO
NATIONAL COUNTIES BUILDING SOCIETY
NATIONAL WESTMINSTER BANK PLC
NATIONWIDE BUILDING SOCIETY

NEWBURY BUILDING SOCIETY
NEWCASTLE BUILDING SOCIETY
NORTHERN BANK LTD
NORTHERN ROCK PLC
NORWICH & PETERBOROUGH BUILDING SOCIETY
PORTMAN BUILDING SOCIETY
PRINCIPALITY BUILDING SOCIETY
REGENTSMEAD LTD
REPUBLIC NATIONAL BANK OF NEW YORK
RIGGS BANK EUROPE LTD
THE ROYAL BANK OF SCOTLAND PLC
SAFFRON WALDEN HERTS & ESSEX BUILDING SOCIETY
SAINSBURY'S BANK
SUN BANK PLC
ULSTER BANK LTD
UNITED ASSET FINANCE LTD
UNITED TRUST BANK LTD
VERNON BUILDING SOCIETY
WINTRUST SECURITIES LTD
YORKSHIRE BANK PLC

RETAIL PROPERTIES
AAREAL BANK
ABBEY NATIONAL PLC
ALLCHURCHES MORTGAGE COMPANY
ALLIANCE & LEICESTER (GIRO BANK)
ALLIED DUNBAR PROVIDENT
ALLIED IRISH BANK
ANGLO IRISH BANK CORPORATION PLC
HENRY ANSBACHER & CO
ARBUTHNOT LATHAM & CO
BHF BANK AG
BALTIC PROPERTY FINANCE PLC
BANK JULIUS BAER & CO
THE BANK OF EAST ASIA
BANK OF SCOTLAND (CENTREBANK)
BANK OF TOKYO – MITSUBISHI
BANK OF WALES PLC
BANKERS TRUST COMPANY
BARCLAYS BANK PLC
BARNSLEY BUILDING SOCIETY
BATH BUILDING SOCIETY
BAYERISCHE VEREINSBANK AG
BIRMINGHAM MIDSHIRES
BRADFORD & BINGLEY PLC
BRISTOL & WEST PLC
BRITISH ARAB COMMERCIAL BANK LTD
THE BRITISH LINEN BANK LTD
BROWN SHIPLEY & CO
CAMBRIDGE BUILDING SOCIETY

CANADA LIFE LTD
CHARTERHOUSE PROPERTY FINANCE LTD
CHASE MANHATTAN, J P MORGAN
CHESHIRE BUILDING SOCIETY
CITIBANK INTERNATIONAL PLC
CITY GROUP
CLOSE BROTHERS LTD
CLYDESDALE BANK
COMMERCIAL ACCEPTANCES
CO-OPERATIVE BANK
COVENTRY BUILDING SOCIETY
CREDIT AGRICOLE INDOSUEZ
CREDIT LYONNAIS
DARLINGTON BUILDING SOCIETY
DEPFA BANK AG
DERBYSHIRE BUILDING SOCIETY
DEUTSCHE BANK AG
DEUTSCHE HYP AG
DEUTSCHE HYPO
DUNBAR GROUP PLC
DUNFERMLINE BUILDING SOCIETY
EAGLE STAR MORTGAGES LTD
ERSTE BANK
EUROHYPO
EXETER BANK
FIRST NATIONAL BANK
FIRST NATIONAL BUILDING SOCIETY
FURNESS BUILDING SOCIETY
G E CAPITAL REAL ESTATE
GOLDMAN SACHS REAL ESTATE PRINCIPAL INVESTMENT
GRANVILLE BANK LTD
HSBC BANK PLC
HAMBURGISCHE LANDESBANK
HAMPSHIRE TRUST PLC
HINCKLEY & RUGBY BUILDING SOCIETY
JULIAN HODGE BANK LTD
HOLBORN SECURITIES PLC
HYPOVEREINSBANK REAL ESTATE CAPITAL
INVESTEC BANK (UK) LTD
KBC BANK NV
KENT RELIANCE BUILDING SOCIETY
LAMBETH BUILDING SOCIETY
LANDESBANK HESSEN-THÜRINGEN (HELABA)
LEEK UNITED BUILDING SOCIETY
LEGAL & GENERAL BANK
LEOPOLD JOSEPH & SONS LTD
LIVERPOOL & VICTORIA
LLOYDS TSB
MANCHESTER BUILDING SOCIETY
W M MANN & CO (INVESTMENTS) LTD

MANSFIELD BUILDING SOCIETY
MARSDEN BUILDING SOCIETY
MERCANTILE BUILDING SOCIETY
MERRILL LYNCH INTERNATIONAL LTD
MIDLAND BANK
J P MORGAN & CO
MORGAN STANLEY DEAN WITTER
NATIONAL COUNTIES BUILDING SOCIETY
NATIONAL WESTMINSTER BANK PLC
NATIONWIDE BUILDING SOCIETY
NEWBURY BUILDING SOCIETY
NEWCASTLE BUILDING SOCIETY
NOMURA BANK INTERNATIONAL
NORDEA
NORTHERN BANK LTD
NORTHERN ROCK PLC
NORWICH & PETERBOROUGH BUILDING SOCIETY
NORWICH UNION PLC
PORTMAN BUILDING SOCIETY
PRINCIPALITY BUILDING SOCIETY
PRUDENTIAL PORTFOLIO MANAGERS LTD
REGENTSMEAD LTD
REPUBLIC NATIONAL BANK OF NEW YORK
RIGGS BANK EUROPE LTD
N M ROTHSCHILD & SONS LTD
THE ROYAL BANK OF SCOTLAND PLC
SAFFRON WALDEN HERTS & ESSEX BUILDING SOCIETY
SANWA BANK
SOCIÉTÉ GÉNÉRALE
SÜDDEUTSCHE BODENCREDIT & HYPOTHEKENBANK AG
SUMITOMO BANK
SUN BANK PLC
SUN LIFE OF CANADA GROUP OF COMPANIES
SVENSKA HANDELSBANKEN
ULSTER BANK LTD
UNION BANK OF SWITZERLAND
UNITED ASSET FINANCE LTD
UNITED BANK OF KUWAIT PLC
UNIVERSAL BUILDING SOCIETY
VERNON BUILDING SOCIETY
UBS WARBURG
WEST BROMWICH BUILDING SOCIETY
WESTDEUTSCHE IMMOBILIEN BANK
THE WESTHYP WESTFÄLISCHE HYPOTHEKENBANK AG
WINTRUST SECURITIES LTD
WÜRTTEMBERGER HYPO
YORKSHIRE BANK PLC

BY MAXIMUM LOAN TO VALUE

These lenders stipulate a ceiling to their lending as a proportion of the value of the property.

100%

BALTIC PROPERTY FINANCE PLC
CITY GROUP
DEUTSCHE BANK AG
GOLDMAN SACHS REAL ESTATE PRINCIPAL INVESTMENT
HYPOVEREINSBANK REAL ESTATE CAPITAL
MERRILL LYNCH INTERNATIONAL LTD

95%

ALLCHURCHES MORTGAGE COMPANY
HENRY ANSBACHER & CO
BATH BUILDING SOCIETY
G E CAPITAL REAL ESTATE
J P MORGAN & CO

90%

CHARTERHOUSE PROPERTY FINANCE LTD
HSBC BANK PLC
RHEINISCHE HYPOTHEKENBANK AG
UNITED TRUST BANK LTD
THE WESTHYP WESTFÄLISCHE HYPOTHEKENBANK AG
WINTRUST SECURITIES LTD

85%

ARREAL BANK
BRISTOL & WEST PLC
CANADA LIFE LTD
CHASE MANHATTAN, J P MORGAN
DEPFA BANK AG
DEUTSCHE HYP AG
EUROHYPO
MANCHESTER BUILDING SOCIETY
MORGAN STANLEY DEAN WITTER
NEWCASTLE BUILDING SOCIETY
UCB GROUP PLC
VERNON BUILDING SOCIETY
WÜRTTEMBERGER HYPO

80%

ABBEY NATIONAL PLC
ALLIANCE & LEICESTER (GIRO BANK)
BHF BANK AG
BARCLAYS BANK PLC
BARNSLEY BUILDING SOCIETY
BRADFORD & BINGLEY PLC
BRITISH ARAB COMMERCIAL BANK LTD

DEUTSCHE HYPO
ERSTE BANK
KBC BANK NV
LANDESBANK HESSEN-THÜRINGEN (HELABA)
LEGAL & GENERAL BANK
NOMURA BANK INTERNATIONAL
NORDEA
NORWICH UNION PLC
PORTMAN BUILDING SOCIETY
SANWA BANK
SÜDDEUTSCHE BODENCREDIT & HYPOTHEKENBANK AG
UBS WARBURG
UNITED BANK OF KUWAIT PLC

75%

ALLIED DUNBAR PROVIDENT
ANGLO IRISH BANK CORPORATION PLC
ARBUTHNOT LATHAM & CO
BANK OF TOKYO – MITSUBISHI
BAYERISCHE VEREINSBANK AG
BIRMINGHAM MIDSHIRES
THE BRITISH LINEN BANK LTD
CAMBRIDGE BUILDING SOCIETY
CHESHIRE BUILDING SOCIETY
CITIBANK INTERNATIONAL PLC
COVENTRY BUILDING SOCIETY
CREDIT AGRICOLE INDOSUEZ
CREDIT LYONNAIS
DUNFERMLINE BUILDING SOCIETY
EAGLE STAR MORTGAGES LTD
FIRST NATIONAL BANK
FIRST NATIONAL BUILDING SOCIETY
FURNESS BUILDING SOCIETY
HSBC BANK PLC
HAMBURGISCHE LANDESBANK
HERITABLE BANK LTD
HINCKLEY & RUGBY BUILDING SOCIETY
JULIAN HODGE BANK LTD
INVESTEC BANK (UK) LTD
LAMBETH BUILDING SOCIETY
MANSFIELD BUILDING SOCIETY
MARSDEN BUILDING SOCIETY
MERCANTILE BUILDING SOCIETY
NEWBURY BUILDING SOCIETY
NORTHERN BANK LTD
NORTHERN ROCK PLC
NORWICH & PETERBOROUGH BUILDING SOCIETY
NORWICH UNION PLC
PRINCIPALITY BUILDING SOCIETY
PRUDENTIAL PORTFOLIO MANAGERS LTD
RIGGS BANK EUROPE LTD

N M ROTHSCHILD & SONS LTD
SAFFRON WALDEN HERTS & ESSEX BUILDING SOCIETY
SINGER & FRIEDLANDER
SOCIÉTÉ GÉNÉRALE
SUMITOMO BANK
SUN BANK PLC
SUN LIFE OF CANADA GROUP OF COMPANIES
SVENSKA HANDELSBANKEN
UNITED ASSET FINANCE LTD
WESTDEUTSCHE IMMOBILIEN BANK
YORKSHIRE BANK PLC

70%
ALLIED IRISH BANK
BANK JULIUS BAER & CO
THE BANK OF EAST ASIA
BANK OF SCOTLAND (CENTREBANK)
BANK OF WALES PLC
CLOSE BROTHERS LTD
CLYDESDALE BANK
COMMERCIAL ACCEPTANCES
DARLINGTON BUILDING SOCIETY
DERBYSHIRE BUILDING SOCIETY
DUNBAR GROUP PLC
GRANVILLE BANK LTD
HAMPSHIRE TRUST PLC
HOLBORN SECURITIES PLC
KENT RELIANCE BUILDING SOCIETY
LEEK UNITED BUILDING SOCIETY
LEOPOLD JOSEPH & SONS LTD
LIVERPOOL & VICTORIA
W M MANN & CO (INVESTMENTS) LTD
NATIONAL COUNTIES BUILDING SOCIETY
NATIONWIDE BUILDING SOCIETY
P L T LTD
THE ROYAL BANK OF SCOTLAND PLC
ULSTER BANK LTD
UNION BANK OF SWITZERLAND
UNIVERSAL BUILDING SOCIETY
WEST BROMWICH BUILDING SOCIETY

65%
BANK LEUMI (UK) PLC
BROWN SHIPLEY & CO
CHELSEA BUILDING SOCIETY
CLYDESDALE BANK
REGENTSMEAD LTD
REPUBLIC NATIONAL BANK OF NEW YORK
SCOTTISH AGRICULTURAL SECURITIES CORPORATION PLC

60%
AGRICULTURAL MORTGAGE CORPORATION PLC
CO-OPERATIVE BANK

BY SIZE OF LOAN (MORE THAN £10M)

These lenders will consider loans of more than £10m.

AAREAL BANK
ABBEY NATIONAL PLC
AGRICULTURAL MORTGAGE CORPORATION PLC
ALLIANCE & LEICESTER (GIRO BANK)
ALLIED IRISH BANK
ANGLO IRISH BANK
BHF BANK AG
BALTIC PROPERTY FINANCE PLC
BANK OF TOKYO – MITSUBISHI
BANK OF WALES
BANKERS TRUST COMPANY
BARCLAYS BANK PLC
BAYERISCHE VEREINSBANK AG
BRADFORD & BINGLEY PLC
BRISTOL & WEST PLC
THE BRITISH LINEN BANK LTD
CANADA LIFE LTD
CHARTERHOUSE PROPERTY FINANCE LTD
CHASE MANHATTAN, J P MORGAN
CITIBANK INTERNATIONAL PLC
CITY GROUP
CLOSE BROTHERS LTD
CLYDESDALE BANK
CO-OPERATIVE BANK
CREDIT AGRICOLE INDOSUEZ
CREDIT LYONNAIS
DEPFA BANK AG
DEUTSCHE BANK AG
DEUTSCHE HYP AG
DEUTSCHE HYPO
ERSTE BANK
EUROHYPO
G E CAPITAL REAL ESTATE
HSBC BANK PLC
HYPOVEREINSBANK REAL ESTATE CAPITAL
INTERMEDIATE CAPITAL GROUP PLC
INVESTEC BANK (UK) LTD
KBC BANK NV
LANDESBANK HESSEN-THÜRINGEN (HELABA)
LEGAL & GENERAL BANK
MERRILL LYNCH INTERNATIONAL LTD
MIDLAND BANK
J P MORGAN & CO
MORGAN STANLEY DEAN WITTER

NATIONAL WESTMINSTER BANK PLC
NATIONWIDE BUILDING SOCIETY
NOMURA BANK INTERNATIONAL
NORDEA
NORTHERN BANK LTD
NORWICH UNION PLC
PORTMAN BUILDING SOCIETY
PRUDENTIAL PORTFOLIO MANAGERS LTD
RHEINISCHE HYPOTHEKENBANK AG
RIGGS BANK EUROPE LTD
N M ROTHSCHILD & SONS
THE ROYAL BANK OF SCOTLAND PLC
SANWA BANK
SOCIÉTÉ GÉNÉRALE
SUMITOMO BANK
SUN LIFE OF CANADA GROUP OF COMPANIES
UBS WARBURG
UCB GROUP PLC
UNION BANK OF SWITZERLAND
UNITED BANK OF KUWAIT PLC
WEST BROMWICH BUILDING SOCIETY
WESTDEUTSCHE IMMOBILIEN BANK
THE WESTHYP WESTFÄLISCHE HYPOTHEKENBANK AG
WÜRTTEMBERGER HYPO
YORKSHIRE BANK PLC

BY MARGIN SPREAD

Minimum margin 1.5% and below

ABBEY NATIONAL PLC	0.25%
AGRICULTURAL MORTGAGE CORPORATION PLC	1.0%
ALLIED IRISH BANK	1.5%
HENRY ANSBACHER & CO	1.5%
BHF BANK AG	0.8%
BANK JULIUS BAER & CO	1.5%
THE BANK OF EAST ASIA	1.0%
BANK OF TOKYO – MITSUBISHI	0.75%
BANK OF WALES PLC	1.0%
BARCLAYS BANK PLC	0.6%
BAYERISCHE VEREINSBANK AG	0.75%
BRADFORD & BINGLEY PLC	1.0%
BRISTOL & WEST PLC	1.25%
BRITISH ARAB COMMERCIAL BANK LTD	1.5%
THE BRITISH LINEN BANK LTD	1.5%
BROWN SHIPLEY & CO	1.0%
CANADA LIFE LTD	1.0%
CHARTERHOUSE PROPERTY FINANCE LTD	1.25%
CHASE MANHATTAN, J P MORGAN	1.0%
CHELSEA BUILDING SOCIETY	1.0%
CITIBANK INTERNATIONAL PLC	1.0%
CITY GROUP	1.0%

CLYDESDALE BANK	1.0%
CREDIT AGRICOLE INDOSUEZ	1.0%
CREDIT LYONNAIS	1.25%
DEPFA BANK AG	0.75%
DEUTSCHE GENOSSENSCHAFTS BANK	1.0%
DEUTSCHE HYP AG	0.8%
DEUTSCHE HYPO	0.75%
ERSTE BANK	0.8%
EUROHYPO	0.75%
G E CAPITAL REAL ESTATE	1.0%
GRANVILLE BANK	1.0%
HSBC BANK PLC	0.8%
HAMBURGISCHE LANDESBANK	0.9%
HINCKLEY & RUGBY BUILDING SOCIETY	0.75%
HOLBORN SECURITIES PLC	0.75%
HYPOVEREINSBANK REAL ESTATE CAPITAL	0.75%
INVESTEC BANK (UK) LTD	1.5%
LANDESBANK HESSEN-THÜRINGEN (HELABA)	1.0%
LEGAL & GENERAL BANK	0.25%
LEOPOLD JOSEPH & SONS LTD	1.5%
LLOYDS TSB	1.0%
MIDLAND BANK	1.0%
NATIONAL WESTMINSTER BANK PLC	0.9%
NOMURA BANK INTERNATIONAL	0.9%
NORDEA	0.25%
NORTHERN BANK LTD	1.0%
NORTHERN ROCK PLC	1.5%
PORTMAN BUILDING SOCIETY	0.9%
PRUDENTIAL PORTFOLIO MANAGERS LTD	1.5%
RHEINISCHE HYPOTHEKENBANK AG	0.6%
RIGGS BANK EUROPE LTD	1.5%
N M ROTHSCHILD & SONS	1.0%
THE ROYAL BANK OF SCOTLAND PLC	1.0%
SANWA BANK	1.0%
SINGER & FRIEDLANDER	0.5%
SOCIÉTÉ GÉNÉRALE	1.0%
SÜDDEUTSCHE BODENCREDIT & HYPOTHEKENBANK AG	1.0%
SUN LIFE OF CANADA GROUP OF COMPANIES	1.5%
SVENSKA HANDELSBANKEN	1.5%
UCB GROUP PLC	1.5%
UNION BANK OF SWITZERLAND	0.8%
UNITED BANK OF KUWAIT PLC	1.25%
WESTDEUTSCHE IMMOBILIEN BANK	0.85%
THE WESTHYP WESTFÄLISCHE HYPOTHEKENBANK AG	0.85%
WÜRTTEMBERGER HYPO	0.75%

COMPANY LISTINGS

Aareal Bank

Paulinenstrasse 15
65189 Wiesbaden
Germany

Tel 00 49 611 348 2885

Fax 00 49 611 348 2757

Contact

Karl Hienz Glauner

Criteria

1	Maximum Loan to Value	85%
2	Benchmark Lending Rate	Libor
3	Margin Spread	70–150 basis points
4	Fixed	Possible
5	Minimum Loan	£10,000,000
6	Maximum Loan	None
7	Arrangement Fee Spread	N/A
8	Minimum Length of Lease Required	Depends
9	Usual Length of Loan	5–10 years
10	Investment	Yes
11	Refinance	Yes
12	Owner Occupier	No
13	Residential Investment	No
14	Development Finance	No
15	Residential Development	No
16	Hotels and Leisure	Yes
17	Healthcare	No
18	Bridging and/or Mezzanine Finance	No

Remarks

Part of the DePfa group.

Abbey National Plc

201 Grafton Gate East
Central Milton Keynes
MK9 1AN

Tel 0870 608 0091

Fax 01908 344 221

Contact

Nigel Shepherd
Nick Hyland

Criteria

1	Maximum Loan to Value	80%
2	Benchmark Lending Rate	Base/Libor
3	Margin Spread	Varies
4	Fixed	Yes
5	Minimum Loan	£50,001
6	Maximum Loan	None
7	Arrangement Fee Spread	0.25%-1.00%
8	Minimum Length of Lease Required	Varies
9	Usual Length of Loan	3-20 years
10	Investment	Yes
11	Refinance	Yes
12	Owner Occupier	Yes
13	Residential Investment	No
14	Development Finance	No
15	Residential Development	No
16	Hotels and Leisure	No
17	Healthcare	No
18	Bridging and/or Mezzanine Finance	No

Agricultural Mortgage Corporation Plc

A M C House
Chantry Street
Andover
Hampshire SP10 1DE

Tel 01264 334344

Fax 01264 334614

Email: info@amcplc.com

Contact

Jon Drew – Customer Relations Manager
Tel: 01264 386238
Jonathan Allright – Marketing Manager
Tel: 01264 386312
John O'Meara – Team Leader – Scotland/North
Tel: 01264 386211
Jim Higgins – Team Leader – Wales & W. Mids
Tel: 01264 386280
Sara Ogilvie – Team Leader – South West
Tel: 01264 386271
Justin Edwards – Team Leader – South East
Tel: 01264 386234

Criteria

1	Maximum Loan to Value	50%
2	Benchmark Lending Rate	Base + 2%
3	Margin Spread	Case specific
4	Fixed	Yes
5	Minimum Loan	£25,001
6	Maximum Loan	None
7	Arrangement Fee Spread	0.5%-1.0%
8	Minimum Length of Lease Required	30 years
9	Usual Length of Loan	5-40 years
10	Investment	Yes
11	Refinance	Yes
12	Owner Occupier	Yes
13	Residential Investment	No
14	Development Finance	Yes
15	Residential Development	No
16	Hotels and Leisure	No
17	Healthcare	No
18	Bridging and/or Mezzanine Finance	No

Remarks

Lends to commercial farming and rural businesses, for any commercial purpose - including diversification projects, build conversions (office developments to holiday lets). In addition to term lending, also now offers working capital facilities. Again these are secured on agricultural property, but allow for money to be drawn, repaid and then redrawn as the customer requires.

Allchurches Mortgage Company

Beaufort House
Brunswick Road
Gloucester
GL1 1JZ

Tel 01452 526265

Fax 01452 311690

Contact

Sue Neish
Tel: 01452 526265 ext 31

Criteria

1	Maximum Loan to Value	95%
2	Benchmark Lending Rate	Standard variable
3	Margin Spread	1%
4	Fixed	No
5	Minimum Loan	£25,001
6	Maximum Loan	£250,000
7	Arrangement Fee Spread	No fee
8	Minimum Length of Lease Required	60 years
9	Usual Length of Loan	25 years
10	Investment	No
11	Refinance	Yes
12	Owner Occupier	Yes
13	Residential Investment	No
14	Development Finance	No
15	Residential Development	No
16	Hotels and Leisure	No
17	Healthcare	No
18	Bridging and/or Mezzanine Finance	No

Remarks

Church of England clergy are its niche market.

Alliance & Leicester (Giro Bank)

62 Hagley Road
Birmingham
B16 8PE

Tel 0121 454 1851

Fax 0121 452 1436

Contact

Stuart Wilson
Paul James
Peter Mole
Tim Jones

Criteria

1	Maximum Loan to Value	80%
2	Benchmark Lending Rate	Base
3	Margin Spread	2%-4%
4	Fixed	Yes
5	Minimum Loan	£15,001
6	Maximum Loan	None
7	Arrangement Fee Spread	1.00%-1.25%
8	Minimum Length of Lease Required	N/A
9	Usual Length of Loan	Up to 10 years
10	Investment	Yes
11	Refinance	Yes
12	Owner Occupier	Yes
13	Residential Investment	No
14	Development Finance	Yes
15	Residential Development	No
16	Hotels and Leisure	No
17	Healthcare	No
18	Bridging and/or Mezzanine Finance	No

Allied Dunbar Provident

9–15 Sackville Street
London
W1A 2JP

Tel 020 7434 3211

Fax 020 7437 9527

Contact

Carroll Raphael
Graham Blanchard

Criteria

1	Maximum Loan to Value	75%
2	Benchmark Lending Rate	3 month Libor
3	Margin Spread	2%-3%
4	Fixed (by way of swap)	Up to 5 years
5	Minimum Loan	£100,000
6	Maximum Loan	£4,000,000
7	Arrangement Fee Spread	0.25%-1%
8	Minimum Length of Lease Required	60 years
9	Usual Length of Loan	5-10 years
10	Investment	Yes
11	Refinance	Yes
12	Owner Occupier	Yes
13	Residential Investment	No
14	Development Finance	No
15	Residential Development	No
16	Hotels and Leisure	No
17	Healthcare	No
18	Bridging and/or Mezzanine Finance	No

Remarks

Lends on all types of commercial property except leisure.

Allied Irish Bank

City Office
12 Old Jewry
London
EC2R 8DP

Tel 020 7606 4900

Fax 020 7606 4966

Contact

Christopher Blowers
Finbarr Daly

Criteria

1	Maximum Loan to Value	70%
2	Benchmark Lending Rate	Bank base/3 month Libor
3	Margin Spread	1.5%-3%
4	Fixed	3/5 years
5	Minimum Loan	£100,000
6	Maximum Loan	£20,000,000
7	Arrangement Fee Spread	0.5%-1%
8	Minimum Length of Lease Required	40 years
9	Usual Length of Loan	1-15 years
10	Investment	Yes
11	Refinance	Yes
12	Owner Occupier	Yes
13	Residential Investment	Yes, buy-to-let package
14	Development Finance	Yes, pre-let and partial pre-let
15	Residential Development	Yes
16	Hotels and Leisure	Yes
17	Healthcare	Yes
18	Bridging and/or Mezzanine Finance	No

Remarks

Lends on all types of commercial property, including leisure, hotels and healthcare.

Anglo Irish Bank Corporation Plc

10 Old Jewry
London
EC2R 8DN

Tel 020 7710 7000

Fax 020 7710 7050

Contact

Ruairi Conneely
Pat O'Hara
Peter Ralph
Jim Springham
John Daly
Barbara Jackson

Criteria

1	Maximum Loan to Value	75%
2	Benchmark Lending Rate	Base/3 month Libor
3	Margin Spread	1.5%-2.5%
4	Fixed	Yes
5	Minimum Loan	£500,000
6	Maximum Loan	None
7	Arrangement Fee Spread	0.5%-1%
8	Minimum Length of Lease Required	N/A
9	Usual Length of Loan	1-6 years
10	Investment	Yes
11	Refinance	Yes
12	Owner Occupier	No
13	Residential Investment	Yes
14	Development Finance	Yes (particularly residential)
15	Residential Development	Yes
16	Hotels and Leisure	Yes
17	Healthcare	Yes
18	Bridging and/or Mezzanine Finance	Yes

Remarks

Speculative residential development. Pre-let commercial development.

Henry Ansbacher & Co

One Mitre Square
London
EC3A 5AN

Tel 020 7283 2500

Fax 020 7626 0850

Contact

P A Cragg
K D Griggs
S R Murrell

Criteria

1	Maximum Loan to Value	95%
2	Benchmark Lending Rate	3 month Libor
3	Margin Spread	1.5%-2%
4	Fixed	Yes
5	Minimum Loan	£500,000
6	Maximum Loan	£5,000,000
7	Arrangement Fee Spread	0.5%-1%
8	Minimum Length of Lease Required	10 years
9	Usual Length of Loan	6 months-5 years
10	Investment	Yes
11	Refinance	Yes
12	Owner Occupier	No
13	Residential Investment	No
14	Development Finance	Yes
15	Residential Development	No
16	Hotels and Leisure	No
17	Healthcare	No
18	Bridging and/or Mezzanine Finance	Yes

Remarks

Mezzanine lending preferred or equity with profits share.

Arab Banking Company

Arab Banking Corporation House
1-5 Moorgate
London
EC2R 6AB

Tel 020 7726 4599

Fax 020 7606 9987

Contact

Jeffrey Applegate

Criteria

1	Maximum Loan to Value	N/A
2	Benchmark Lending Rate	N/A
3	Margin Spread	N/A
4	Fixed	N/A
5	Minimum Loan	N/A
6	Maximum Loan	N/A
7	Arrangement Fee Spread	N/A
8	Minimum Length of Lease Required	N/A
9	Usual Length of Loan	N/A
10	Investment	N/A
11	Refinance	N/A
12	Owner Occupier	N/A
13	Residential Investment	N/A
14	Development Finance	N/A
15	Residential Development	N/A
16	Hotels and Leisure	N/A
17	Healthcare	N/A
18	Bridging and/or Mezzanine Finance	N/A

Remarks

The company only lends to its existing client base and its own property fund.

Arbuthnot Latham & Co

Royex House
Aldermanbury Square
London
EC2V 7NU

Tel 020 7418 7200

Fax 020 7454 0114

Contact

Stewart Barnes

Criteria

1	Maximum Loan to Value	75%
2	Benchmark Lending Rate	Lloyds Bank base
3	Margin Spread	2.0%-4.0%
4	Fixed	No
5	Minimum Loan	£100,000
6	Maximum Loan	£5,000,000
7	Arrangement Fee Spread	1%
8	Minimum Length of Lease Required	30 years remaining
9	Usual Length of Loan	1-3 years
10	Investment	Yes
11	Refinance	No
12	Owner Occupier	Yes
13	Residential Investment	No
14	Development Finance	Yes
15	Residential Development	Yes
16	Hotels and Leisure	Yes
17	Healthcare	Yes
18	Bridging and/or Mezzanine Finance	Yes

Remarks

Will lend development finance but only in the southeast. Speculative development considered on its merits.

BHF Bank AG

61 Queen Street
London
EC4R 1AE

Tel 020 7634 2300/2378

Fax 020 7248 5739

Contact

Salman Hasan
Tony Whetstone

Criteria

1	Maximum Loan to Value	90%
2	Benchmark Lending Rate	Libor
3	Margin Spread	0.80%
4	Fixed	Yes
5	Minimum Loan	£3,000,000
6	Maximum Loan	None
7	Arrangement Fee Spread	0.5%
8	Minimum Length of Lease Required	None
9	Usual Length of Loan	5 years
10	Investment	Yes
11	Refinance	Yes
12	Owner Occupier	Yes
13	Residential Investment	Yes
14	Development Finance	Yes
15	Residential Development	Yes
16	Hotels and Leisure	Yes
17	Healthcare	No
18	Bridging and/or Mezzanine Finance	Yes

Remarks

Will consider all quality transactions including speculative development for qualified parties.

Baltic Property Finance Plc

25/26 Albemarle Street
London
W1S 4AD

Tel 020 7255 7500

Fax 020 7491 8678

Contact

Robert Black

Criteria

1	Maximum Loan to Value	100%
2	Benchmark Lending Rate	Barclays base
3	Margin Spread	Varies
4	Fixed	No
5	Minimum Loan	£300,000
6	Maximum Loan	£6,000,000
7	Arrangement Fee Spread	Varies
8	Minimum Length of Lease Required	Varies
9	Usual Length of Loan	Up to 3 years
10	Investment	No
11	Refinance	Yes
12	Owner Occupier	Yes
13	Residential Investment	No
14	Development Finance	Yes
15	Residential Development	No
16	Hotels and Leisure	No
17	Healthcare	No
18	Bridging and/or Mezzanine Finance	Yes

Remarks

Baltic is an entrepreneurial joint venture organisation providing mezzanine/equity for transactions that are potentially value enhancing.

Bank Julius Baer & Co

Bevis Marks House
Bevis Marks
London
EC3A 7NE

Tel 020 7623 4211

Fax 020 7283 6146

Contact

John Grist

Criteria

1	Maximum Loan to Value	75%
2	Benchmark Lending Rate	3 month Libor
3	Margin Spread	1.5%-3%
4	Fixed	No
5	Minimum Loan	£500,000
6	Maximum Loan	£2,000,000
7	Arrangement Fee Spread	0.5%-1%
8	Minimum Length of Lease Required	30 years
9	Usual Length of Loan	3-5 years
10	Investment	Yes
11	Refinance	Yes
12	Owner Occupier	Yes
13	Residential Investment	Yes
14	Development Finance	No
15	Residential Development	Yes
16	Hotels and Leisure	Yes
17	Healthcare	No
18	Bridging and/or Mezzanine Finance	Yes

Bank Leumi (UK) Plc

20 Stratford Place
London
W1N 9AF

Fax 020 7907 8192

Contact

David Griffiths
Tel: 020 7907 8116
Malcolm Bloom
Tel: 020 7907 8184

Criteria

1	Maximum Loan to Value	66%
2	Benchmark Lending Rate	Base/Libor
3	Margin Spread	2%–3%
4	Fixed	No
5	Minimum Loan	£500,000
6	Maximum Loan	£8,000,000
7	Arrangement Fee Spread	1%
8	Minimum Length of Lease Required	None
9	Usual Length of Loan	Up to 3 years
10	Investment	Sometimes
11	Refinance	Sometimes
12	Owner Occupier	No
13	Residential Investment	Yes
14	Development Finance	Yes
15	Residential Development	Yes
16	Hotels and Leisure	Sometimes
17	Healthcare	No
18	Bridging and/or Mezzanine Finance	Yes

Remarks

Short-term bridging and enablement finance, primarily for developments or breakup. Commercial developments should normally be pre-let.

Bank of America

PO Box 407
Bank of America House
1 Alie Street
London
E1 8DE

Tel 020 7634 4282

Fax 020 7634 4690

Contact

Dermot J McMullan

Criteria

1	Maximum Loan to Value	N/A
2	Benchmark Lending Rate	N/A
3	Margin Spread	N/A
4	Fixed	N/A
5	Minimum Loan	N/A
6	Maximum Loan	N/A
7	Arrangement Fee Spread	N/A
8	Minimum Length of Lease Required	N/A
9	Usual Length of Loan	N/A
10	Investment	N/A
11	Refinance	N/A
12	Owner Occupier	N/A
13	Residential Investment	N/A
14	Development Finance	N/A
15	Residential Development	N/A
16	Hotels and Leisure	N/A
17	Healthcare	N/A
18	Bridging and/or Mezzanine Finance	N/A

Remarks

Bank of America is the largest real estate lender in the USA. Currency lending to existing clients only. However, changes will be likely following the merger with Nationsbank.

The Bank of East Asia

75 Shaftesbury Avenue
London
W1V 8BB

Tel 020 7208 3812
020 7208 3811

Fax 020 7734 0523

Contact

Arnold Cho
Kenneth Tam

Criteria

1	Maximum Loan to Value	70%
2	Benchmark Lending Rate	Bank base/3 month Libor
3	Margin Spread	1%-3%
4	Fixed	Yes
5	Minimum Loan	£30,000
6	Maximum Loan	£2,000,000
7	Arrangement Fee Spread	0.5%
8	Minimum Length of Lease Required	Varies
9	Usual Length of Loan	10-15 years
10	Investment	Yes
11	Refinance	Yes
12	Owner Occupier	Yes
13	Residential Investment	Yes
14	Development Finance	No
15	Residential Development	Yes
16	Hotels and Leisure	Yes
17	Healthcare	Yes
18	Bridging and/or Mezzanine Finance	No

Remarks

Principally lends to expatriate Chinese in residential and retail sectors.

Bank of Scotland (Centrebank)

Corporate Banking
Teviot House
41 South Gyle Crescent
Edinburgh
EH12 9BG

Tel 0131 442 5080
0131 442 7777
0131 317 5707

Fax 0131 317 5952

Contact

Gordon Smith
Sarah Boyd
Robert Low
Alastair Campbell

Criteria

1	Maximum Loan to Value	70%
2	Benchmark Lending Rate	Bank base rate
3	Margin Spread	2%–3%
4	Fixed	Yes
5	Minimum Loan	£150,000
6	Maximum Loan	None
7	Arrangement Fee Spread	0.5%–1%
8	Minimum Length of Lease Required	25 years plus length of loan
9	Usual Length of Loan	5–25 years or retirement
10	Investment	Yes
11	Refinance	Yes
12	Owner Occupier	Yes
13	Residential Investment	Yes, through one broker only
14	Development Finance	No
15	Residential Development	No
16	Hotels and Leisure	Yes
17	Healthcare	Yes
18	Bridging and/or Mezzanine Finance	No

Remarks

Looks at proposals through a panel of 10 brokers.

Bank of Tokyo – Mitsubishi

12–15 Finsbury Circus
London
EC2M 7BT

Tel 020 7577 1717

Fax 020 7577 1759

Contact

Alistair Mackie

Criteria

1	Maximum Loan to Value	75%
2	Benchmark Lending Rate	3 month Libor
3	Margin Spread	0.75%-2%
4	Fixed	Yes
5	Minimum Loan	£5,000,000
6	Maximum Loan	None
7	Arrangement Fee Spread	0.25%-0.75%
8	Minimum Length of Lease Required	Flexible
9	Usual Length of Loan	5-10 years
10	Investment	Yes
11	Refinance	Yes
12	Owner Occupier	Yes
13	Residential Investment	No
14	Development Finance	Yes
15	Residential Development	No
16	Hotels and Leisure	No
17	Healthcare	No
18	Bridging and/or Mezzanine Finance	Yes

Bank of Wales Plc

One Kingsway
Cardiff
CF10 4YB

Tel 02920 800800

Fax 02920 800804

Email: whitet@bankofwales.co.uk

Contact

T. White
P. Williams

Criteria

1	Maximum Loan to Value	80%
2	Benchmark Lending Rate	Libor/Base
3	Margin Spread	1.0%-2.5%
4	Fixed	Yes
5	Minimum Loan	£250,000
6	Maximum Loan	None
7	Arrangement Fee Spread	Up to 1%
8	Minimum Length of Lease Required	None
9	Usual Length of Loan	1-25 years
10	Investment	Yes
11	Refinance	Yes
12	Owner Occupier	Yes
13	Residential Investment	Yes
14	Development Finance	Yes
15	Residential Development	Yes
16	Hotels and Leisure	Yes
17	Healthcare	Yes
18	Bridging and/or Mezzanine Finance	No

Bankers Trust Company

Real Estate Investment Bank Group
1 Appold Street
Broadgate
London
EC2A 2HE

Tel 020 7982 2500/1593

Fax 020 7982 1593/3308

Contact

Alistair Dixon
Tel: 020 7982 3714
Richard Mully
Tel: 020 7982 2745
George Kountouris
Tel: 020 7982 2549
Gary Wilder

Criteria

1	Maximum Loan to Value	Providers of mezzanine debt
2	Benchmark Lending Rate	Base
3	Margin Spread	Varied
4	Fixed	No
5	Minimum Loan	£3,000,000
6	Maximum Loan	£25,000,000
7	Arrangement Fee Spread	Varies
8	Minimum Length of Lease Required	None
9	Usual Length of Loan	3-5 years
10	Investment	Yes
11	Refinance	Yes
12	Owner Occupier	Yes
13	Residential Investment	No
14	Development Finance	No
15	Residential Development	No
16	Hotels and Leisure	No
17	Healthcare	No
18	Bridging and/or Mezzanine Finance	Yes

Remarks

Bankers Trust aims to adopt a structured approach to the provision of mezzanine finance to enable the borrower to achieve enhanced returns. Providers of mezzanine and equity debt only.

Banque Nationale de Paris Plc

8-13 King William Street
London
EC4P 4HS

Tel 020 7283 9514

Fax 020 7929 0310

Contact

Keith Bennett

Criteria

1	Maximum Loan to Value	N/A
2	Benchmark Lending Rate	N/A
3	Margin Spread	N/A
4	Fixed	N/A
5	Minimum Loan	N/A
6	Maximum Loan	N/A
7	Arrangement Fee Spread	N/A
8	Minimum Length of Lease Required	N/A
9	Usual Length of Loan	N/A
10	Investment	N/A
11	Refinance	N/A
12	Owner Occupier	N/A
13	Residential Investment	N/A
14	Development Finance	N/A
15	Residential Development	N/A
16	Hotels and Leisure	N/A
17	Healthcare	N/A
18	Bridging and/or Mezzanine Finance	N/A

Remarks

The bank still administers its existing loan book but is not writing new business.

Barclays Bank Plc

54 Lombard Street
London
EC3P 3AH

Tel 020 7699 2755

Fax 020 7699 3882

Email: andy.chaplin@barclays.co.uk

Contact

Andy Chaplin

Criteria

1	Maximum Loan to Value	80% for commercial mortgages. Special scheme available for doctors. 70% for property investment
2	Benchmark Lending Rate	Base/Libor
3	Margin Spread	1%–5% normal
4	Fixed	Yes
5	Minimum Loan	£15,000
6	Maximum Loan	Unlimited
7	Arrangement Fee Spread	Negotiable
8	Minimum Length of Lease Required	Negotiable
9	Usual Length of Loan	Up to 25 years commercial mortgage Up to 20 years residential property investment Up to 10 years commercial property investment
10	Investment	Yes
11	Refinance	Yes
12	Owner Occupier	Yes
13	Residential Investment	Yes
14	Development Finance	Yes
15	Residential Development	Yes
16	Hotels and Leisure	Yes
17	Healthcare	Yes
18	Bridging and/or Mezzanine Finance	Yes

Barclays Property Team

54 Lombard Street
London
EC3P 3AH

Tel 020 7699 5000

Fax 0870 242 2754/020 7699 3882

Contact

Alan Connell – Head of Property Team
Richard Payne – Head of Structured Finance
Nick Salisbury – PFI
Steve Amos – Housing Association Finance & Local Authority Finance

Criteria

1	Maximum Loan to Value	80% (possibly more for pre-sold developments)
2	Benchmark Lending Rate	Libor
3	Margin Spread	0.6%-2%
4	Fixed	Yes
5	Minimum Loan	£2,000,000
6	Maximum Loan	None
7	Arrangement Fee Spread	0.4%-1%
8	Minimum Length of Lease Required	Varies
9	Usual Length of Loan	Up to 3 years for development finance Up to 10 years for investment finance
10	Investment	Yes
11	Refinance	Yes
12	Owner Occupier	Yes
13	Residential Investment	Yes
14	Development Finance	Yes
15	Residential Development	Yes
16	Hotels and Leisure	Yes
17	Healthcare	No
18	Bridging and/or Mezzanine Finance	Yes

Remarks

Cashflow based project or portfolio financings for commercial/residential property and hotels. Private finance initiative and housing associations. Will judge deals on a case by case basis.

Barnsley Building Society

Permanent Building
Regent Street
Barnsley
S70 2EH

Tel 01226 733999

Fax 01226 287374

Contact

Ian Alderman

Criteria

1	Maximum Loan to Value	80%
2	Benchmark Lending Rate	Standard variable rate
3	Margin Spread	Up to 2%
4	Fixed	Yes
5	Minimum Loan	£15,001
6	Maximum Loan	£1,500,000
7	Arrangement Fee Spread	1%
8	Minimum Length of Lease Required	N/A
9	Usual Length of Loan	5-25 years
10	Investment	Yes
11	Refinance	Yes
12	Owner Occupier	Yes
13	Residential Investment	No
14	Development Finance	No
15	Residential Development	No
16	Hotels and Leisure	No
17	Healthcare	No
18	Bridging and/or Mezzanine Finance	No

Bath Building Society

20 Charles Street
Bath
BA1 1HY

Tel 01225 423271
01225 475702

Fax 01225 446914

Contact

Mrs Alison Hodgman
Tel: 01225 475702

Criteria

1	Maximum Loan to Value	95%
2	Benchmark Lending Rate	Standard variable rate
3	Margin Spread	1.5%-2.5%
4	Fixed	No
5	Minimum Loan	£30,000
6	Maximum Loan	£1,000,000
7	Arrangement Fee Spread	£100
8	Minimum Length of Lease Required	75 years
9	Usual Length of Loan	5-25 years
10	Investment	Yes
11	Refinance	Yes
12	Owner Occupier	Yes
13	Residential Investment	Yes
14	Development Finance	No
15	Residential Development	Sometimes
16	Hotels and Leisure	Yes
17	Healthcare	Yes
18	Bridging and/or Mezzanine Finance	No

Remarks

50-mile radius of Bath.

Bayerische Vereinsbank AG

1 Royal Exchange Buildings
London
EC3V 3LD

Zentralbereich Immobilienfinanzierung-Ausland
Am Tücherpark 16
80311 München
Germany

Tel 020 7626 1301
Fax 020 7696 9989

Tel 00 49 89 3782 2716
Fax 00 49 89 3782 9389

Contact

Ray Daws (London)
Manuela Better
(Germany)

Criteria

1	Maximum Loan to Value	75%
2	Benchmark Lending Rate	Libor
3	Margin Spread	0.75%-1.5%
4	Fixed	Yes
5	Minimum Loan	£2,000,000
6	Maximum Loan	£15,000,000
7	Arrangement Fee Spread	0.25%-0.75%
8	Minimum Length of Lease Required	N/A
9	Usual Length of Loan	Up to 10 years
10	Investment	Yes
11	Refinance	Yes
12	Owner Occupier	Yes
13	Residential Investment	No
14	Development Finance	Yes, pre-let
15	Residential Development	No
16	Hotels and Leisure	No
17	Healthcare	No
18	Bridging and/or Mezzanine Finance	Yes

Birmingham Midshires

Business & Professional Finance
PO Box 81
Pendeford Business Park
Wobaston Road
Wolverhampton
WV9 5HZ

Tel 01902 302817
01902 325588

Fax 01902 325510
01902 325590

Contact

Maggie Taylor
Business Development
Tel: 01902 325588

Criteria

1	Maximum Loan to Value	80%
2	Benchmark Lending Rate	3 month Libor
3	Margin Spread	1%-2.5%
4	Fixed	Yes
5	Minimum Loan	£100,000
6	Maximum Loan	£10,000,000
7	Arrangement Fee Spread	Negotiable
8	Minimum Length of Lease Required	N/A
9	Usual Length of Loan	25 years max. 5 years min.
10	Investment	Yes
11	Refinance	Yes
12	Owner Occupier	Yes
13	Residential Investment	No
14	Development Finance	Yes
15	Residential Development	No
16	Hotels and Leisure	Yes
17	Healthcare	Yes
18	Bridging and/or Mezzanine Finance	No

Remarks

Now part of the Halifax Group.

Bradford & Bingley Plc

Property Finance
PO Box 88
Crossflatts
Bingley
West Yorkshire
BD16 2UA

Tel 01274 554188/554798

Fax 01274 544195

Contact

Liz Walker
Emma Bates

Criteria

1	Maximum Loan to Value	80%
2	Benchmark Lending Rate	Libor
3	Margin Spread	Negotiable
4	Fixed	Up to 10 years
5	Minimum Loan	£250,000
6	Maximum Loan	None
7	Arrangement Fee Spread	0.25%-1%
8	Minimum Length of Lease Required	N/A
9	Usual Length of Loan	2-25 years
10	Investment	Yes
11	Refinance	Yes
12	Owner Occupier	No
13	Residential Investment	No
14	Development Finance	No
15	Residential Development	No
16	Hotels and Leisure	No
17	Healthcare	No
18	Bridging and/or Mezzanine Finance	No

Bristol & West Plc

PO Box 27
One Temple Quay
Bristol
BS99 7AX

Tel 0117 943 2531

Fax 0117 929 3814

Contact

Brian Cherry
Paul Selley
Colin MacLaran
David Nicholson

Criteria

1	Maximum Loan to Value	85%
2	Benchmark Lending Rate	3 month Libor/Swaps
3	Margin Spread	0.85%-1.5%
4	Fixed	Yes, 1-10 years
5	Minimum Loan	£500,000
6	Maximum Loan	£50,000,000
7	Arrangement Fee Spread	0.25%-0.5%
8	Minimum Length of Lease Required	End of mortgage term
9	Usual Length of Loan	3-20 years
10	Investment	Yes
11	Refinance	Yes
12	Owner Occupier	No
13	Residential Investment	Yes
14	Development Finance	No
15	Residential Development	No
16	Hotels and Leisure	No
17	Healthcare	No
18	Bridging and/or Mezzanine Finance	No

British Arab Commercial Bank Ltd

8/10 Mansion House Place
London
EC4N 8BJ

Tel 020 7648 7777

Fax 020 7648 7779

Email: steve.maltby@bacb.co.uk

Contact

Stephen Maltby
Manager Lending
& Marketing
Tel: 020 7972 6357

Criteria

1	Maximum Loan to Value	75%
2	Benchmark Lending Rate	Libor
3	Margin Spread	1%+
4	Fixed	Yes
5	Minimum Loan	£1,000,000
6	Maximum Loan	£15,000,000
7	Arrangement Fee Spread	Negotiable
8	Minimum Length of Lease Required	N/A
9	Usual Length of Loan	5 years
10	Investment	Yes
11	Refinance	Yes
12	Owner Occupier	No
13	Residential Investment	No
14	Development Finance	No
15	Residential Development	No
16	Hotels and Leisure	No
17	Healthcare	No
18	Bridging and/or Mezzanine Finance	No

The British Linen Bank Ltd

8 Fredericks Place
London
EC2R 8AT

Tel 020 7601 6840

Fax 020 7600 1383

Contact

Ian Mitchelmore
Andrew Darling

Criteria

1	Maximum Loan to Value	75%
2	Benchmark Lending Rate	Libor
3	Margin Spread	1.5%-3%
4	Fixed	Yes
5	Minimum Loan	£1,000,000
6	Maximum Loan	None
7	Arrangement Fee Spread	Up to 1%
8	Minimum Length of Lease Required	Variable
9	Usual Length of Loan	Up to 10 years
10	Investment	Yes
11	Refinance	Yes
12	Owner Occupier	Yes
13	Residential Investment	Yes
14	Development Finance	No
15	Residential Development	No
16	Hotels and Leisure	No
17	Healthcare	No
18	Bridging and/or Mezzanine Finance	No

Remarks

Good quality investment (commercial) preferred.

Brown Shipley & Co

Founders Court
Lothbury
London
EC2R 7HE

Tel 020 7606 9833

Fax 020 7606 4825

Contact

Robert Smoker
Jon Watson

Criteria

1	Maximum Loan to Value	66%
2	Benchmark Lending Rate	3 month Libor
3	Margin Spread	1.5%-2.0%
4	Fixed	Yes
5	Minimum Loan	£500,000
6	Maximum Loan	£3,000,000
7	Arrangement Fee Spread	0.25%-1.5%
8	Minimum Length of Lease Required	50 years
9	Usual Length of Loan	1 day-7 years amortising
10	Investment	Yes
11	Refinance	Yes
12	Owner Occupier	Yes
13	Residential Investment	Yes
14	Development Finance	Yes, pre-let only
15	Residential Development	No
16	Hotels and Leisure	No
17	Healthcare	No
18	Bridging and/or Mezzanine Finance	No

Cambridge Building Society

51 Newmarket Road
Cambridge
CB5 8FF

Tel 01223 727727

Fax 01223 727700

Contact

Andrew Pepperell
Andrew Buck
Chris Green

Criteria

1	Maximum Loan to Value	75%
2	Benchmark Lending Rate	Own residential base rate
3	Margin Spread	Base-2.5%
4	Fixed	No
5	Minimum Loan	£25,000
6	Maximum Loan	£1,000,000
7	Arrangement Fee Spread	0.5%-1%
8	Minimum Length of Lease Required	25 years plus length of loan
9	Usual Length of Loan	5-25 years
10	Investment	Yes
11	Refinance	Yes
12	Owner Occupier	Yes
13	Residential Investment	Yes
14	Development Finance	Yes
15	Residential Development	Yes
16	Hotels and Leisure	Yes
17	Healthcare	Yes
18	Bridging and/or Mezzanine Finance	No

Remarks

Commercial lending only provided on property within a 30-mile radius of Cambridge.

Canada Life Ltd

Martin House
Martin Lane
London
EC4R 0DP

Tel 020 7955 0155

Fax 020 7955 0150

Contact

John Garlick
Wendy Tyreman
Nicholas Bent

Criteria

1	Maximum Loan to Value	85%
2	Benchmark Lending Rate	Swap
3	Margin Spread	80 basis points
4	Fixed	Yes, 10–30 years
5	Minimum Loan	£3,000,000
6	Maximum Loan	£30,000,000
7	Arrangement Fee Spread	0.25%-0.5%
8	Minimum Length of Lease Required	10 years
9	Usual Length of Loan	10–30 years
10	Investment	Yes
11	Refinance	Yes
12	Owner Occupier	No
13	Residential Investment	No
14	Development Finance	No
15	Residential Development	No
16	Hotels and Leisure	Yes
17	Healthcare	No
18	Bridging and/or Mezzanine Finance	No

Remarks

The company grants long-term fixed interest loans on good quality commercial property. Five-year floating rate loans are also available.

Capital Home Loans Ltd

PO Box 151
Fleet
Hampshire
GU13 8YF

Tel 01252 812271

Fax 01252 811826

Contact

David Guinane – Managing Director
Michael Barbour – Head of Operations
Mark Wilson – Head of Sales and Marketing

Criteria

1	Maximum Loan to Value	90%
2	Benchmark Lending Rate	Libor/Bank base
3	Margin Spread	Varies
4	Fixed	Yes
5	Minimum Loan	£15,001
6	Maximum Loan	£500,000
7	Arrangement Fee Spread	0.25%-1%
8	Minimum Length of Lease Required	Varies
9	Usual Length of Loan	25 years
10	Investment	No
11	Refinance	Residential only
12	Owner Occupier	Yes
13	Residential Investment	Yes
14	Development Finance	No
15	Residential Development	No
16	Hotels and Leisure	No
17	Healthcare	No
18	Bridging and/or Mezzanine Finance	No

Remarks

The residential investment side focuses primarily on housing associations.

Charterhouse Property Finance Ltd

1 Paternoster Row
St Pauls
London
EC4M 7DH

Tel 020 7248 4000

Fax 020 7246 2110

Contact

Andrew Moffat
Tel: 020 7246 2255
Philip Jeffcock
Tel: 020 7246 2023
Natalie Howard
Tel: 020 7246 2436
Toby Szpiro
Tel: 020 7246 2108
Andrew Macland
Tel: 020 7246 2517

Criteria

1	Maximum Loan to Value	90%
2	Benchmark Lending Rate	3 month Libor
3	Margin Spread	1.25%-3%
4	Fixed	Yes
5	Minimum Loan	£1,000,000
6	Maximum Loan	None
7	Arrangement Fee Spread	0.25%-1.5%
8	Minimum Length of Lease Required	Varies
9	Usual Length of Loan	3 months-5 years
10	Investment	Yes
11	Refinance	Yes
12	Owner Occupier	No
13	Residential Investment	Yes
14	Development Finance	Yes
15	Residential Development	No
16	Hotels and Leisure	No
17	Healthcare	No
18	Bridging and/or Mezzanine Finance	Yes

Remarks

Prepared to actively participate in some transactions. Specialises in high loan to value and also offers mezzanine facilities.

Chase Manhattan, J P Morgan

25 Copthall Avenue
London
EC2R 7DR

Tel 020 7638 5858

Fax 020 7256 5036

Contact

Christopher King – Director
Andrew Haines – Manager
Steve Machin – Manager

Criteria

1	Maximum Loan to Value	85% investment 100% pre-let/ sold development
2	Benchmark Lending Rate	Libor
3	Margin Spread	1%-2.5% pa
4	Fixed	Yes
5	Minimum Loan	£3,000,000
6	Maximum Loan	None
7	Arrangement Fee Spread	0.5%-1.0%
8	Minimum Length of Lease Required	15 years
9	Usual Length of Loan	3-7 years
10	Investment	Yes
11	Refinance	Yes
12	Owner Occupier	Yes
13	Residential Investment	No
14	Development Finance	Yes, only pre-let or pre-sold
15	Residential Development	No
16	Hotels and Leisure	Yes
17	Healthcare	No
18	Bridging and/or Mezzanine Finance	Yes

Chelsea Building Society

Thirlestaine Hall
Thirlestaine Road
Cheltenham
Gloucester
GL53 7AL

Tel 01242 271271

Fax 01242 571441

Contact

David Richards –
Mortgage Practice
Manager
Tel: 01242 271428

Criteria

1	Maximum Loan to Value	95%
2	Benchmark Lending Rate	Standard variable rate 6.34%
3	Margin Spread	N/A
4	Fixed	N/A
5	Minimum Loan	£20,000
6	Maximum Loan	£1,000,000
7	Arrangement Fee Spread	N/A
8	Minimum Length of Lease Required	55 years
9	Usual Length of Loan	5-25 years
10	Investment	N/A
11	Refinance	N/A
12	Owner Occupier	Yes
13	Residential Investment	Yes
14	Development Finance	No
15	Residential Development	No
16	Hotels and Leisure	N/A
17	Healthcare	N/A
18	Bridging and/or Mezzanine Finance	No

Cheltenham & Gloucester Plc

Barnett Way
Gloucester
GL4 7RL

Tel 01452 372372

Fax 01452 375879

Contact

Brian Harwood

Criteria

1	Maximum Loan to Value	N/A
2	Benchmark Lending Rate	N/A
3	Margin Spread	N/A
4	Fixed	N/A
5	Minimum Loan	N/A
6	Maximum Loan	N/A
7	Arrangement Fee Spread	N/A
8	Minimum Length of Lease Required	N/A
9	Usual Length of Loan	N/A
10	Investment	N/A
11	Refinance	N/A
12	Owner Occupier	N/A
13	Residential Investment	N/A
14	Development Finance	N/A
15	Residential Development	N/A
16	Hotels and Leisure	N/A
17	Healthcare	N/A
18	Bridging and/or Mezzanine Finance	N/A

Remarks

The commercial department is only lending to existing clients.

Cheshire Building Society

Castle Street
Macclesfield
Cheshire
SK11 6AF

Tel 01625 613612

Fax 01625 617147

Contact

Brian Dickinson

Criteria

1	Maximum Loan to Value	75%
2	Benchmark Lending Rate	Standard variable rate
3	Margin Spread	0.5%
4	Fixed	Yes
5	Minimum Loan	£15,001
6	Maximum Loan	£1,000,000
7	Arrangement Fee Spread	1%
8	Minimum Length of Lease Required	None
9	Usual Length of Loan	5-20 years
10	Investment	Yes
11	Refinance	Yes
12	Owner Occupier	Yes
13	Residential Investment	Yes
14	Development Finance	No
15	Residential Development	No
16	Hotels and Leisure	Yes
17	Healthcare	Yes
18	Bridging and/or Mezzanine Finance	No

Citibank International Plc

Citibank Business & Commercial
St Martins House
1 Hammersmith Grove
London
W6 0NY

Tel 020 7500 3127

Fax 020 7500 3591

Contact

Alastair Caie

Criteria

1	Maximum Loan to Value	75% (100% healthcare)
2	Benchmark Lending Rate	Bank base
3	Margin Spread	1%–3.5%
4	Fixed	Sometimes
5	Minimum Loan	£100,000
6	Maximum Loan	£10,000,000
7	Arrangement Fee Spread	1%
8	Minimum Length of Lease Required	99 years
9	Usual Length of Loan	5–25 years
10	Investment	Yes
11	Refinance	Yes
12	Owner Occupier	Yes, healthcare only
13	Residential Investment	Yes
14	Development Finance	No
15	Residential Development	No
16	Hotels and Leisure	No
17	Healthcare	Yes
18	Bridging and/or Mezzanine Finance	No

City Group

Victoria Plaza
111 Buckingham Palace Road
London
SW1W 0SB

Tel 020 7721 2000

Fax 020 7721 2834

Contact

Ken Beisser
Robert Balick
Nigel King

Criteria

1	Maximum Loan to Value	100% subject to status or income stream
2	Benchmark Lending Rate	Base
3	Margin Spread	Varies
4	Fixed	No
5	Minimum Loan	£6,000,000
6	Maximum Loan	None
7	Arrangement Fee Spread	Varies
8	Minimum Length of Lease Required	None
9	Usual Length of Loan	Generally short-term lending
10	Investment	Yes
11	Refinance	Yes
12	Owner Occupier	Yes
13	Residential Investment	No
14	Development Finance	Yes
15	Residential Development	Yes
16	Hotels and Leisure	Yes
17	Healthcare	No
18	Bridging and/or Mezzanine Finance	Yes

Remarks

Formerly Salomon Brothers. Has extensive experience in financing of office buildings, hotels, resorts, industrial facilities, shopping centres and development sites throughout Europe. Provides customised investment banking service for many types of investor including property companies.

Close Brothers Ltd

10 Crown Place
London
EC2A 4FT

Tel 020 7655 3100

Fax 020 7247 1205

Contact

Frank Pennal –
Senior Manager
Tel: 020 7655 3443
Robert Orr –
Senior Manager
Tel: 020 7655 3412
Jonathan Smith –
Senior Manager
Tel: 020 7655 3779

Criteria

1	Maximum Loan to Value	70%
2	Benchmark Lending Rate	Libor
3	Margin Spread	3%–4%
4	Fixed	Yes
5	Minimum Loan	£50,000
6	Maximum Loan	£10,000,000
7	Arrangement Fee Spread	1%–1.5%
8	Minimum Length of Lease Required	No minimum – provided spread
9	Usual Length of Loan	1–5 years
10	Investment	Yes
11	Refinance	Yes
12	Owner Occupier	No
13	Residential Investment	Yes
14	Development Finance	Yes
15	Residential Development	Yes
16	Hotels and Leisure	No
17	Healthcare	No
18	Bridging and/or Mezzanine Finance	Yes – Bridging No – Mezzanine

Remarks

For loans of £50–£500,000 contact: Tim Noble Tel: 020 7655 3771, Tony Redondo Tel: 020 7655 3769, Jane Reeve Tel: 020 7655 3772.
For loans of £500,000–£10,000,000 see under Contact.
Lends on development with repayment date. Also residential and commercial development. The latter predominantly pre-let. Lends on secondary investment portfolios with good interest cover.

Clydesdale Bank

Contact

Contact the commercial mortgage manager at nearest branch concerned. To obtain branch address and number call: 0141 248 7070

Criteria

1	Maximum Loan to Value	70%
2	Benchmark Lending Rate	Bank/Libor
3	Margin Spread	1%-5%
4	Fixed	Sometimes
5	Minimum Loan	£15,000
6	Maximum Loan	None
7	Arrangement Fee Spread	0.5%-1%
8	Minimum Length of Lease Required	20 years
9	Usual Length of Loan	1-20 years
10	Investment	Yes
11	Refinance	Yes
12	Owner Occupier	Yes
13	Residential Investment	Yes
14	Development Finance	Yes
15	Residential Development	Yes
16	Hotels and Leisure	Yes
17	Healthcare	Yes
18	Bridging and/or Mezzanine Finance	No

Commercial Acceptances

Hall Studio
23B Grove End Road
London
NW8 9BP

Tel 020 7289 3326

Fax 020 7286 9280

Contact

Neville Freed
L B Brown
D A Hertz

Criteria

1	Maximum Loan to Value	70%
2	Benchmark Lending Rate	Bank base
3	Margin Spread	3%
4	Fixed	No
5	Minimum Loan	£25,000
6	Maximum Loan	£4,000,000
7	Arrangement Fee Spread	1%, refundable
8	Minimum Length of Lease Required	60 years
9	Usual Length of Loan	1 day–6 months
10	Investment	Yes
11	Refinance	Yes
12	Owner Occupier	Yes
13	Residential Investment	Yes
14	Development Finance	Pre-let only
15	Residential Development	Yes
16	Hotels and Leisure	No
17	Healthcare	No
18	Bridging and/or Mezzanine Finance	Yes

Remarks

Specialises in bridging finance from 1 day to 6 months.
Likes deals where quick reaction is required.

Co-operative Bank

PO Box 101
1 Balloon Street
Manchester
M60 4EP

Tel 0161 829 5349

Fax 0161 839 8284

Contact

Commercial Mortgage Manager at nearest branch

Criteria

1	Maximum Loan to Value	60%
2	Benchmark Lending Rate	Bank base
3	Margin Spread	2.5%-5%
4	Fixed	Yes
5	Minimum Loan	Varies
6	Maximum Loan	None
7	Arrangement Fee Spread	1%-1.5%
8	Minimum Length of Lease Required	35 years
9	Usual Length of Loan	1-10 years
10	Investment	Yes
11	Refinance	Yes
12	Owner Occupier	Yes
13	Residential Investment	No
14	Development Finance	No
15	Residential Development	No
16	Hotels and Leisure	Yes
17	Healthcare	Yes
18	Bridging and/or Mezzanine Finance	No

Coventry Building Society

Economic House
PO Box 9
High Street
Coventry
CV1 5QN

Tel 0845 766 5522

Contact

Nigel Kay

Criteria

1	Maximum Loan to Value	75%
2	Benchmark Lending Rate	Building Society base rate
3	Margin Spread	Varies
4	Fixed	Yes
5	Minimum Loan	£25,000
6	Maximum Loan	£500,000
7	Arrangement Fee Spread	1%
8	Minimum Length of Lease Required	N/A
9	Usual Length of Loan	5-25 years
10	Investment	Yes
11	Refinance	No
12	Owner Occupier	No
13	Residential Investment	Yes
14	Development Finance	No
15	Residential Development	No
16	Hotels and Leisure	No
17	Healthcare	No
18	Bridging and/or Mezzanine Finance	No

Remarks

Lending in 50-mile radius of Coventry.

Credit Agricole Indosuez

122 Leadenhall Street
London
EC2V 4QH

Tel 020 7971 4000

Fax 020 7971 4406

Contact

Nicola Crumpton
Peter Stevens

Criteria

1	Maximum Loan to Value	75%
2	Benchmark Lending Rate	Libor
3	Margin Spread	1%-2%
4	Fixed	Yes
5	Minimum Loan	£2,000,000
6	Maximum Loan	£15,000,000
7	Arrangement Fee Spread	0.25%-0.75%
8	Minimum Length of Lease Required	10 years
9	Usual Length of Loan	1-5 years
10	Investment	Yes
11	Refinance	Yes
12	Owner Occupier	Sometimes
13	Residential Investment	No
14	Development Finance	No
15	Residential Development	No
16	Hotels and Leisure	No
17	Healthcare	No
18	Bridging and/or Mezzanine Finance	No

Remarks

Lending to existing clients only.

Credit Lyonnais

PO Box 81
Broadwalk House
5 Appold Street
London
EC2A 2JP

Tel 020 7374 4014

Fax 020 7214 7159

Contact

David Brewster
Alan Grey
Graham Thomas

Criteria

1	Maximum Loan to Value	75%
2	Benchmark Lending Rate	Libor
3	Margin Spread	1.25%-3%
4	Fixed	Yes
5	Minimum Loan	£3,000,000
6	Maximum Loan	None
7	Arrangement Fee Spread	0.5%-1%
8	Minimum Length of Lease Required	5 years plus length of loan
9	Usual Length of Loan	1-5 years
10	Investment	Yes
11	Refinance	Yes
12	Owner Occupier	Yes
13	Residential Investment	No
14	Development Finance	Yes
15	Residential Development	No
16	Hotels and Leisure	No
17	Healthcare	No
18	Bridging and/or Mezzanine Finance	No

Darlington Building Society

Sentinel House
Lingfield Way
Darlington
Co Durham

Tel 01325 366366

Fax 01325 741000

Contact

D C Christie ARICS –
Commercial Manager
Tel: ext 3156
R W Murphy MBA
DMS MIMgt –
Underwriting Manager
Tel: ext 3114

Criteria

1	Maximum Loan to Value	70%
2	Benchmark Lending Rate	Building Society standard variable rate
3	Margin Spread	0.5%-2.5%
4	Fixed	Yes - minimum £500,000
5	Minimum Loan	£25,100
6	Maximum Loan	£1,000,000
7	Arrangement Fee Spread	0.5%-1.0%
8	Minimum Length of Lease Required	To exceed mortgage term
9	Usual Length of Loan	5-25 years
10	Investment	Yes
11	Refinance	Yes
12	Owner Occupier	Yes
13	Residential Investment	Yes
14	Development Finance	No
15	Residential Development	No
16	Hotels and Leisure	Some
17	Healthcare	Some
18	Bridging and/or Mezzanine Finance	No

Remarks

South Durham/North Yorks area only.

DePfa Bank AG

London Branch
38 Lombard Street
London
EC3V 9BS

Paulinenstrasse 15
65189 Wiesbaden
Germany

Tel 020 7456 9200
Fax 020 7929 5055

Tel 00 49 611 348 2885
Fax 00 49 611 348 2757

Contact

Francis Hazeel
Charles Balch
Sue Whitehorne
Paul Stone
Paul Stoneham

Criteria

1	Maximum Loan to Value	85%-90%
2	Benchmark Lending Rate	Cost of funds/Libor
3	Margin Spread	70-150 basis points
4	Fixed	Requirement for hedging
5	Minimum Loan	Investment (bipartite) £5,000,000 Investment (club) and speculative £10,000,000
6	Maximum Loan	N/A
7	Arrangement Fee Spread	30-125 bp
8	Minimum Length of Lease Required	Varies
9	Usual Length of Loan	5-10 years
10	Investment	Yes
11	Refinance	Yes
12	Owner Occupier	Yes
13	Residential Investment	No
14	Development Finance	Yes
15	Residential Development	No
16	Hotels and Leisure	Yes
17	Healthcare	No
18	Bridging and/or Mezzanine Finance	-

Remarks

DePfa specialises in a diverse range of property services from large senior debt transactions to mezzanine finance and investment banking business. Most of DePfa's business has been mortgage based in the past, but it is able to lend corporately or against the security of shares. DePfa finances all the main property types, with an emphasis on commercial, retail and warehouse/distribution.

In equity-style deals, the loans can be smaller than the normal lending criteria, i.e. in the £2.5-£5m range.

Derbyshire Building Society

Duffield Hall
Duffield
Derby
DE56 1AG

Tel 01332 841000

Fax 01332 844666

Email: geoff.gullon@thederbyshire.co.uk

Contact

Geoff Gullon,
Mortgage Risks Officer
Tel: 01332 844353
Malcolm Sinclair,
Manager, Lending
Development & Risk
Tel: 01332 844762
Bob Pearman,
Manager, Centre
Processing Unit
Tel: 01332 841000
ext 2519

Criteria

1	Maximum Loan to Value	70%
2	Benchmark Lending Rate	Building Society cost of funds
3	Margin Spread	1%-3%
4	Fixed	Yes
5	Minimum Loan	£100,000
6	Maximum Loan	None
7	Arrangement Fee Spread	1%
8	Minimum Length of Lease Required	50 years plus length of loan
9	Usual Length of Loan	5-25 years
10	Investment	Yes
11	Refinance	Yes
12	Owner Occupier	Yes
13	Residential Investment	Yes
14	Development Finance	No
15	Residential Development	No
16	Hotels and Leisure	No
17	Healthcare	Yes
18	Bridging and/or Mezzanine Finance	No

Deutsche Bank AG

Winchester House
1 Great Winchester Street
London EC2N 2DB

Tel 020 7545 8000

Fax 020 7545 7130

Contact

Neil Lawson-May
Paul Rivlin

Criteria

1	Maximum Loan to Value	None, can be up to 100% subject to cashflow etc.
2	Benchmark Lending Rate	3 month Libor
3	Margin Spread	Varies
4	Fixed	Yes
5	Minimum Loan	£25,000,000
6	Maximum Loan	None
7	Arrangement Fee Spread	Varies
8	Minimum Length of Lease Required	Varies
9	Usual Length of Loan	1 month–25 years
10	Investment	Yes
11	Refinance	Yes
12	Owner Occupier	No
13	Residential Investment	No
14	Development Finance	Yes, pre-let
15	Residential Development	No
16	Hotels and Leisure	No
17	Healthcare	No
18	Bridging and/or Mezzanine Finance	Yes

Remarks

Deutsche Bank bases lending decisions on the calibre of the borrower, the quality of the covenant, the property and the cashflow.

Deutsche Genossenschafts Hypothekenbank

Rosen Straße
20095 Hamburg
Germany

Tel 00 49 40 30 10 30
00 49 40 30 10 3935

Fax 00 49 40 30 10 3175

Contact

Frau Brumshagen

Criteria

1	Maximum Loan to Value	75%
2	Benchmark Lending Rate	3 month Libor
3	Margin Spread	1%-1.5%
4	Fixed	Yes
5	Minimum Loan	£1,000,000
6	Maximum Loan	None
7	Arrangement Fee Spread	0.25%-0.75%
8	Minimum Length of Lease Required	Freehold only
9	Usual Length of Loan	10-25 years
10	Investment	Yes
11	Refinance	No
12	Owner Occupier	No
13	Residential Investment	No
14	Development Finance	Pre-let only
15	Residential Development	No
16	Hotels and Leisure	No
17	Healthcare	No
18	Bridging and/or Mezzanine Finance	No

Deutsche Hyp AG

Taunusanlage 9
60329 Frankfurt am Main
Germany

One Love Lane
London
EC2V 7JJ

Tel 00 49 69 254 86438
Fax 00 49 69 254 86404

Tel 020 7600 7575(UK)
Fax 020 7600 7676 (UK)

Contact

Michael Kröger (D)
Robert Baskeyfield (UK)
Andrew Jarrold (UK)

Criteria

1	Maximum Loan to Value	85%
2	Benchmark Lending Rate	Cost of funds or short-term Libor
3	Margin Spread	0.8%-1.5%
4	Fixed	Yes, up to 15 years
5	Minimum Loan	£4,000,000
6	Maximum Loan	£65,000,000
7	Arrangement Fee Spread	0.25%-0.75%
8	Minimum Length of Lease Required	Occupational leases minimum 10 years, or a term 2 years past the facility expiry date, long leasehold minimum 60 years
9	Usual Length of Loan	3-20 years
10	Investment	Yes
11	Refinance	Yes
12	Owner Occupier	Only for clients of first-class financial standing
13	Residential Investment	Only for larger residential apartment blocks with short leases
14	Development Finance	On a case by case basis for substantially (minimum 80%) pre-let developments
15	Residential Development	No
16	Hotels and Leisure	No
17	Healthcare	No
18	Bridging and/or Mezzanine Finance	No

Remarks

Prefers to lend on good commercial properties in quality locations, major cities preferred. Debt service must be fully covered by net rental income, single asset transactions or portfolios. Lends to established property investors. Property finance in all European Community countries.

Deutsche Hypo

City Tower - Level 19
40 Basinghall Street
London
EC2V 5DE

Tel 020 7920 0100

Fax 020 7920 0110

Contact

Walter W Love
Chris Hunter

Criteria

1	Maximum Loan to Value	80%
2	Benchmark Lending Rate	Libor
3	Margin Spread	0.80%-1.20%
4	Fixed	Yes
5	Minimum Loan	£5,000,000
6	Maximum Loan	£50,000,000
7	Arrangement Fee Spread	0.2%-0.5%
8	Minimum Length of Lease Required	5 years
9	Usual Length of Loan	3-10 years
10	Investment	Yes
11	Refinance	Yes
12	Owner Occupier	Yes
13	Residential Investment	Yes
14	Development Finance	Pre-let only
15	Residential Development	Yes
16	Hotels and Leisure	No
17	Healthcare	No
18	Bridging and/or Mezzanine Finance	No

Dunbar Group Plc

9-15 Sackville Street
London
W1A 2JP

Tel 020 7437 7844

Fax 020 7437 3953

Contact

Paul Keay -
Loans Director
Nigel Jackson -
Loans Director
Steve Dry -
Lending Manager

Criteria

1	Maximum Loan to Value	70%
2	Benchmark Lending Rate	Dunbar Bank base rate/ 3 month Libor
3	Margin Spread	2%–4%
4	Fixed	Yes
5	Minimum Loan	£100,000
6	Maximum Loan	£20,000,000
7	Arrangement Fee Spread	1%
8	Minimum Length of Lease Required	50 years
9	Usual Length of Loan	Up to 5 years
10	Investment	Yes
11	Refinance	Yes
12	Owner Occupier	No
13	Residential Investment	Yes
14	Development Finance	Yes
15	Residential Development	Yes
16	Hotels and Leisure	No
17	Healthcare	No
18	Bridging and/or Mezzanine Finance	No

Remarks

Regional offices in Birmingham, Manchester, Leeds, Newcastle, Glasgow.

Dunfermline Building Society

Caledonia House
Carnegie Avenue
Dunfermline
Fife
KY11 5PJ

Tel 01383 627727

Fax 01383 627800

Contact

George Blyth

Criteria

1	Maximum Loan to Value	75%
2	Benchmark Lending Rate	Building society cost of funds
3	Margin Spread	1%-3%
4	Fixed	Yes
5	Minimum Loan	£2,000
6	Maximum Loan	£250,000
7	Arrangement Fee Spread	1%
8	Minimum Length of Lease Required	30 years plus length of loan
9	Usual Length of Loan	5-20 years
10	Investment	Yes
11	Refinance	Yes
12	Owner Occupier	Yes
13	Residential Investment	Yes
14	Development Finance	Yes
15	Residential Development	Yes
16	Hotels and Leisure	Yes
17	Healthcare	Yes
18	Bridging and/or Mezzanine Finance	No

Remarks

Regional lender specialising in Scotland and North of England.

Eagle Star Mortgages Ltd

Eagle Star Centre
Montpellier Drive
Cheltenham
Glos
GL53 7LQ

Tel 01242 221311

Fax 01242 221554

Contact

Brian Cosgrove

Criteria

1	Maximum Loan to Value	75%
2	Benchmark Lending Rate	Libor
3	Margin Spread	1%-1.5%
4	Fixed	No
5	Minimum Loan	£250,000
6	Maximum Loan	£2,500,000
7	Arrangement Fee Spread	1%
8	Minimum Length of Lease Required	60 years
9	Usual Length of Loan	5-25 years
10	Investment	Yes
11	Refinance	Yes
12	Owner Occupier	No
13	Residential Investment	No
14	Development Finance	No
15	Residential Development	No
16	Hotels and Leisure	No
17	Healthcare	No
18	Bridging and/or Mezzanine Finance	No

Erste Bank

68 Cornhill
London
EC3V 3QE

Tel 020 7621 5000

Fax 020 7283 7142

Contact

Richard Mansfield,
Head of Commercial Property
Tel: 020 7621 5018
rmm@erstebank.com
Andrew Goodbody,
Manager, Commercial Property
Tel: 020 7621 5069
arg@erstebank.com

Criteria

1	Maximum Loan to Value	80% for senior debt 90%-95% for senior mezzanine debt
2	Benchmark Lending Rate	Libor
3	Margin Spread	1.0%-1.75%
4	Fixed	Yes
5	Minimum Loan	£5,000,000 (for senior debt)
6	Maximum Loan	£15,000,000 (for senior debt)
7	Arrangement Fee Spread	Varies
8	Minimum Length of Lease Required	None
9	Usual Length of Loan	5-10 years
10	Investment	Yes
11	Refinance	Yes
12	Owner Occupier	No
13	Residential Investment	No
14	Development Finance	Yes, pre-let and part pre-let
15	Residential Development	No
16	Hotels and Leisure	No
17	Healthcare	No
18	Bridging and/or Mezzanine Finance	Yes (see Remarks)

Remarks

Pre-let and part pre-let development considered for parties with strong track records and business plan.
Providers of mezzanine debt (as part of combined senior/mezzanine debt facility).

Eurohypo

Winchester House
1 Great Winchester Street
London
EC2N 2DB

Tel 020 7545 2111

Fax 020 7545 2092

Contact

Steven M Williamson
Director – Head of Marketing
Tel: 020 7545 4152

Criteria

1	Maximum Loan to Value	80%
2	Benchmark Lending Rate	Cost of funds
3	Margin Spread	Typically 0.85%-1.25%
4	Fixed	Yes
5	Minimum Loan	£10,000,000 investment £20,000,000 development
6	Maximum Loan	None
7	Arrangement Fee Spread	0.35%-1.00%
8	Minimum Length of Lease Required	60 years
9	Usual Length of Loan	5-15 years
10	Investment	Yes
11	Refinance	Yes
12	Owner Occupier	Only for clients with first-class covenant
13	Residential Investment	See comments under 15-17
14	Development Finance	Yes
15	Residential Development	Not core areas of business
16	Hotels and Leisure	but considers proposals on
17	Healthcare	their merits
18	Bridging and/or Mezzanine Finance	Yes – via Deutsche Bank

Exeter Bank

Exeter Trust House
Blackboy Road
Exeter
EX4 6SE

Tel 01392 50635
01438 744676

Fax 01392 77798
01438 744625

Contact

Lending Division now run by Sun Bank
Mark Hiscox
Paul Clark

Criteria

1	Maximum Loan to Value	N/A
2	Benchmark Lending Rate	N/A
3	Margin Spread	N/A
4	Fixed	N/A
5	Minimum Loan	N/A
6	Maximum Loan	N/A
7	Arrangement Fee Spread	N/A
8	Minimum Length of Lease Required	N/A
9	Usual Length of Loan	N/A
10	Investment	N/A
11	Refinance	N/A
12	Owner Occupier	N/A
13	Residential Investment	N/A
14	Development Finance	N/A
15	Residential Development	N/A
16	Hotels and Leisure	N/A
17	Healthcare	N/A
18	Bridging and/or Mezzanine Finance	N/A

Remarks

All commercial lending through parent: Sun Bank Plc.

First National Bank

College Road
Harrow
Middx
HA1 1FB

Tel 020 8861 1313

Fax 020 8861 4540

Contact

Jeff Watson
A Turzynski

Criteria

1	Maximum Loan to Value	75%
2	Benchmark Lending Rate	Finance House base rate 3 month Libor
3	Margin Spread	2.5%-4.5%
4	Fixed	No
5	Minimum Loan	£25,000
6	Maximum Loan	£1,000,000
7	Arrangement Fee Spread	Varies
8	Minimum Length of Lease Required	40 years
9	Usual Length of Loan	Up to 25 years
10	Investment	Yes
11	Refinance	Yes
12	Owner Occupier	Yes
13	Residential Investment	Yes
14	Development Finance	No
15	Residential Development	No
16	Hotels and Leisure	No
17	Healthcare	No
18	Bridging and/or Mezzanine Finance	No

Remarks

A commercial property lending subsidiary of Abbey National Plc.

First National Building Society

Sketan House
Booterstown
Co Dublin
Ireland

Tel 00 3531 288 5211

Fax 00 3531 288 5300

Contact

Chris Heard

Criteria

1	Maximum Loan to Value	75%
2	Benchmark Lending Rate	Standard variable rate
3	Margin Spread	Up to 2.5%
4	Fixed	Yes
5	Minimum Loan	£15,001
6	Maximum Loan	£1,000,000
7	Arrangement Fee Spread	1%
8	Minimum Length of Lease Required	75 years
9	Usual Length of Loan	10–30 years
10	Investment	Yes
11	Refinance	Yes
12	Owner Occupier	Yes
13	Residential Investment	Yes
14	Development Finance	No
15	Residential Development	Yes
16	Hotels and Leisure	Yes
17	Healthcare	Yes
18	Bridging and/or Mezzanine Finance	No

Remarks

Irish Republic only.

Furness Building Society

51–55 Duke Street
Barrow-in-Furness
Cumbria
LA14 1RT

Tel 01229 824 560

Fax 01229 837 043

Contact

B Greenwood

Criteria

1	Maximum Loan to Value	75%
2	Benchmark Lending Rate	Cost of funds
3	Margin Spread	1%-2%
4	Fixed	Yes
5	Minimum Loan	None
6	Maximum Loan	£250,000
7	Arrangement Fee Spread	1%
8	Minimum Length of Lease Required	N/A
9	Usual Length of Loan	5-25 years
10	Investment	Yes
11	Refinance	Yes
12	Owner Occupier	Yes
13	Residential Investment	Yes
14	Development Finance	Pre-let only
15	Residential Development	No
16	Hotels and Leisure	Yes
17	Healthcare	No
18	Bridging and/or Mezzanine Finance	No

Remarks

Within 100-mile radius of Barrow-in-Furness.

G E Capital Real Estate

Commercial Property Financing
Clarges House
6-12 Clarges Street
London W1J 8DH

Tel 020 7302 6262

Fax 020 7302 6830

Contact

Scott Parsons
Tel: 020 7302 6264
Simon Farnsworth
Tel: 020 7302 6246
Chris Bates
Tel: 020 7302 6340
Paul Robinson
Tel: 020 7302 6274

Criteria

1	Maximum Loan to Value	90% + (in exceptional cases)
2	Benchmark Lending Rate	Libor
3	Margin Spread	1%-1.75%
4	Fixed	Yes
5	Minimum Loan	£5,000,000; small equity transactions considered
6	Maximum Loan	None
7	Arrangement Fee Spread	0.5%
8	Minimum Length of Lease Required	Varies
9	Usual Length of Loan	3-7 years
10	Investment	Yes
11	Refinance	Yes
12	Owner Occupier	No
13	Residential Investment	Yes
14	Development Finance	No
15	Residential Development	No
16	Hotels and Leisure	No
17	Healthcare	No
18	Bridging and/or Mezzanine Finance	Yes

Remarks

GE Capital is a highly flexible lender. It funds transactions without syndication, is prepared to make equity/mezzanine investments and senior debt finance. Smaller equity transactions may also be considered.

Goldman Sachs Real Estate Principal Investment

Peterborough Court
133 Fleet Street
London
EC3A 2ED

Tel 020 7774 1000

Fax 020 7774 4123

Contact

James Del Favero
Richard Georgi

Criteria

1	Maximum Loan to Value	100% subject to status
2	Benchmark Lending Rate	Base
3	Margin Spread	Varies
4	Fixed	No
5	Minimum Loan	£20,000,000
6	Maximum Loan	None
7	Arrangement Fee Spread	Varies
8	Minimum Length of Lease Required	None
9	Usual Length of Loan	Varies
10	Investment	Yes
11	Refinance	Yes
12	Owner Occupier	Yes
13	Residential Investment	No
14	Development Finance	Yes
15	Residential Development	No
16	Hotels and Leisure	Yes
17	Healthcare	No
18	Bridging and/or Mezzanine Finance	Yes

Remarks

Provides funding for major property investments and developments to recognised and established companies.

Granville Bank Ltd

Mint House
77 Mansell Street
London
E1 8AF

Tel 020 7488 1212

Fax 020 7709 0346

Contact

Tony Redondo
Tim Noble

Criteria

1	Maximum Loan to Value	70%
2	Benchmark Lending Rate	Bank's own base rate (currently 8.25% pa)
3	Margin Spread	3%–6% over own base rate
4	Fixed	No
5	Minimum Loan	£50,001
6	Maximum Loan	£1,000,000
7	Arrangement Fee Spread	1%–2%
8	Minimum Length of Lease Required	35 years
9	Usual Length of Loan	3 months–5 years
10	Investment	Yes
11	Refinance	Yes
12	Owner Occupier	Yes
13	Residential Investment	Yes
14	Development Finance	Yes
15	Residential Development	Yes
16	Hotels and Leisure	Yes
17	Healthcare	Yes
18	Bridging and/or Mezzanine Finance	Yes

Remarks

Specialises in provision of short-term residential bridging and development finance (new build, conversions and refurbishments) and residential and commercial investment properties in England and Wales only. Will always use own independent valuers and solicitors and, where applicable, quantity surveyors. Will discuss most cases. An 'in principle' decision given without delay.

HSBC Bank Plc

Corporate & Institutional Banking
27–32 Poultry
London
EC2P 2BX

Tel 020 7638 2366

Fax 020 7260 0085

Contact

Wendell Harris –
Head of Property
& Construction Finance
Keith Lupton
David Taylor
Mike O'Connor –
Hotels
Steve Bullock
Ian Dunn
James Wade

Criteria

1	Maximum Loan to Value	75%
2	Benchmark Lending Rate	Interbank/Base
3	Margin Spread	0.8%-2.5%
4	Fixed	Yes
5	Minimum Loan	£5-10,000,000
6	Maximum Loan	None
7	Arrangement Fee Spread	0.25%-1%
8	Minimum Length of Lease Required	None
9	Usual Length of Loan	5-7 years
10	Investment	Yes
11	Refinance	Yes
12	Owner Occupier	No
13	Residential Investment	Yes
14	Development Finance	Yes
15	Residential Development	Yes
16	Hotels and Leisure	Yes
17	Healthcare	No
18	Bridging and/or Mezzanine Finance	Yes

Remarks

Prefers lending on portfolios.

Hamburgische Landesbank

Moorgate Hall
155 Moorgate
London
EC2M 6XB

Tel 020 7972 9292

Fax 020 7972 6418

Contact

Joachim Lawrence

Criteria

1	Maximum Loan to Value	75%
2	Benchmark Lending Rate	Cost of funds
3	Margin Spread	0.9%-1.75%
4	Fixed	Yes
5	Minimum Loan	£2,500,000
6	Maximum Loan	None
7	Arrangement Fee Spread	Varies
8	Minimum Length of Lease Required	None
9	Usual Length of Loan	5-20 years
10	Investment	Yes
11	Refinance	Yes
12	Owner Occupier	Only for clients of first-class financial standing
13	Residential Investment	No
14	Development Finance	Pre-let only
15	Residential Development	No
16	Hotels and Leisure	No
17	Healthcare	No
18	Bridging and/or Mezzanine Finance	No

Hampshire Trust Plc

Fareham House
69 High Street
Fareham
Hants
PO16 7BB

Tel 01329 234294

Fax 01329 285910

Contact

Trevor Jones
Steven Dixon

Criteria

1	Maximum Loan to Value	70%
2	Benchmark Lending Rate	11%
3	Margin Spread	0%–3.5% over. Average 2.5%.
4	Fixed	Not available
5	Minimum Loan	£25,000
6	Maximum Loan	£350,000
7	Arrangement Fee Spread	1%–1.5%
8	Minimum Length of Lease Required	50 years plus loan term
9	Usual Length of Loan	3 months–20 years
10	Investment	Yes
11	Refinance	Yes
12	Owner Occupier	Yes
13	Residential Investment	Yes
14	Development Finance	Yes
15	Residential Development	Yes
16	Hotels and Leisure	Yes
17	Healthcare	Yes
18	Bridging and/or Mezzanine Finance	Yes

Remarks

All applications are individually assessed without recourse to credit scoring or the like. Prompt decisions given. Adverse credit and limited accounting information are viewed sympathetically. A high-speed bridging loan facility is available.

Heritable Bank Ltd

52 Berkeley Square
London
W1J 5BD

Tel 020 7493 6621

Fax 020 7629 1958

Email: info@heritable.co.uk

Website: www.heritable.co.uk

Contact

Nick Barrett
Simon White
Graeme Walker

Criteria

1	Maximum Loan to Value	75% of costs
2	Benchmark Lending Rate	H Bank base rate
3	Margin Spread	2.5%-4%
4	Fixed	Yes
5	Minimum Loan	£250,000
6	Maximum Loan	£8,000,000
7	Arrangement Fee Spread	0.5%-1%
8	Minimum Length of Lease Required	None
9	Usual Length of Loan	Up to 36 months
10	Investment	No
11	Refinance	Yes
12	Owner Occupier	No
13	Residential Investment	Yes
14	Development Finance	Yes - residential and commercial
15	Residential Development	Yes
16	Hotels and Leisure	No
17	Healthcare	No
18	Bridging and/or Mezzanine Finance	Yes

Remarks

The Bank lends to all types of residential development throughout England.

Hinckley & Rugby Building Society

81 Upper Bond Street
Hinckley
Leicester
LE10 1DG

Tel 01455 251234

Fax 01455 636237

Contact

Martyn Shortland
Julie Chapman

Criteria

1	Maximum Loan to Value	75%
2	Benchmark Lending Rate	Base mortgage rate + 1.5%
3	Margin Spread	1.5%-2%
4	Fixed	No
5	Minimum Loan	£25,000
6	Maximum Loan	£250,000
7	Arrangement Fee Spread	None
8	Minimum Length of Lease Required	75 years from date of advance
9	Usual Length of Loan	Up to 15 years
10	Investment	Yes
11	Refinance	Possible
12	Owner Occupier	Yes
13	Residential Investment	Yes
14	Development Finance	No
15	Residential Development	No
16	Hotels and Leisure	No
17	Healthcare	No
18	Bridging and/or Mezzanine Finance	No

Remarks

Commercial lending restricted to society's core business area in the East Midlands.

Julian Hodge Bank Ltd

10 Windsor Place
Cardiff
CF1 3BX

Tel 029 2022 0800

Fax 029 2034 4061

Contact

James Penman
George Benjamin
Andrew Silk

Criteria

1	Maximum Loan to Value	75%
2	Benchmark Lending Rate	Bank base
3	Margin Spread	2%–4%
4	Fixed	Yes
5	Minimum Loan	£250,000
6	Maximum Loan	£5,000,000
7	Arrangement Fee Spread	1%
8	Minimum Length of Lease Required	15 years
9	Usual Length of Loan	No minimum – 20 years
10	Investment	Yes
11	Refinance	Yes
12	Owner Occupier	Yes
13	Residential Investment	No
14	Development Finance	Yes
15	Residential Development	Yes
16	Hotels and Leisure	No
17	Healthcare	Yes, doctors and dentists
18	Bridging and/or Mezzanine Finance	No

Holborn Securities Plc

3 Park Road
Regents Park
London
NW1 6AS

Tel 020 7616 6616

Fax 020 7616 6610

Email: central@csc.co.uk

Contact

Henry Ejdelbaum
Glenn Roberts

Criteria

1	Maximum Loan to Value	70%
2	Benchmark Lending Rate	Libor base
3	Margin Spread	2%-5%
4	Fixed	No
5	Minimum Loan	£26,000
6	Maximum Loan	£250,000
7	Arrangement Fee Spread	0.75%-1.5%
8	Minimum Length of Lease Required	N/A
9	Usual Length of Loan	N/A
10	Investment	Yes
11	Refinance	Yes
12	Owner Occupier	Yes
13	Residential Investment	Yes
14	Development Finance	Yes
15	Residential Development	Yes
16	Hotels and Leisure	Yes
17	Healthcare	Yes
18	Bridging and/or Mezzanine Finance	Yes

Remarks

Prefers bridging loans and enablement finance.

HypoVereinsbank Real Estate Capital

110 Cannon Street
London
EC4N 6EW

Tel 020 7573 8212

Fax 020 7573 8706

Contact

Mike Riley
John Humberstone
Peter Scott

Criteria

1	Maximum Loan to Value	100%
2	Benchmark Lending Rate	Libor
3	Margin Spread	0.75%-1.75%
4	Fixed	Yes
5	Minimum Loan	£5,000,000
6	Maximum Loan	None
7	Arrangement Fee Spread	0.25%-1.0%
8	Minimum Length of Lease Required	N/A
9	Usual Length of Loan	2-12 years
10	Investment	Yes
11	Refinance	Yes
12	Owner Occupier	No
13	Residential Investment	Yes
14	Development Finance	Commercial only. Yes, pre-let or partially pre-let only
15	Residential Development	Yes
16	Hotels and Leisure	Yes
17	Healthcare	No
18	Bridging and/or Mezzanine Finance	Yes

Remarks

Will judge deals on case by case basis. If conditions are right, may lend more than 85% loan to value. Will also consider joint ventures and can provide mezzanine finance.

Intermediate Capital Group Plc

62–63 Threadneedle Street
London
EC2R 8HE

Tel 020 7628 9898

Fax 020 7628 2268

Contact

Tom Bartlam

Criteria

1	Maximum Loan to Value	Mezzanine finance and equity finance only
2	Benchmark Lending Rate	Base
3	Margin Spread	Varies
4	Fixed	No
5	Minimum Loan	£4,500,000
6	Maximum Loan	None
7	Arrangement Fee Spread	Varies
8	Minimum Length of Lease Required	None
9	Usual Length of Loan	Short-term funding
10	Investment	No
11	Refinance	No
12	Owner Occupier	No
13	Residential Investment	No
14	Development Finance	Yes, but only leisure
15	Residential Development	No
16	Hotels and Leisure	Yes
17	Healthcare	Yes
18	Bridging and/or Mezzanine Finance	Yes

Remarks

Providers of mezzanine and equity finance as well as immediate capital for buyouts. Primarily active in leisure, hotels and nursing homes. No pure property.

Investec Bank (UK) Ltd

2 Gresham Street
London
EC2V 7QP

Tel 020 7597 4436

Fax 020 7597 4441

Contact

Steven Cook
Gary Dobson
Jill Hagland
Peter Harris
John Pollington
Andrew Scotting

Criteria

1	Maximum Loan to Value	c. 70% but negotiable
2	Benchmark Lending Rate	3 month Libor/Base rate
3	Margin Spread	1.5%-3%
4	Fixed	Yes, max. 5 years
5	Minimum Loan	£300,000
6	Maximum Loan	£40,000,000
7	Arrangement Fee Spread	Negotiable
8	Minimum Length of Lease Required	Varies (short leases considered)
9	Usual Length of Loan	3 months-15 years
10	Investment	Yes
11	Refinance	Yes
12	Owner Occupier	No
13	Residential Investment	Yes
14	Development Finance	London and M25 vicinity. Other prime England locations considered.
15	Residential Development	Yes
16	Hotels and Leisure	No
17	Healthcare	No
18	Bridging and/or Mezzanine Finance	Yes

Remarks

In commercial investment sector, only strong covenants or prime locations considered. Mezzanine funding considered on residential development up to 90% for 'exit fee' arrangements. Offshore structures acceptable.

KBC Bank NV

Exchange House
Primrose Street
London EC2A 2HQ

Tel 020 7638 5812

Fax 020 7663 0151

Email: jstuart.farnell@kbc.be

Contact

Stephen Picton-Pegg
Tel: 020 7256 4866
Stuart Farnell
Tel: 020 7256 4849

Criteria

1	Maximum Loan to Value	80%
2	Benchmark Lending Rate	Libor
3	Margin Spread	1%-2.5%
4	Fixed	Yes
5	Minimum Loan	£3,000,000
6	Maximum Loan	£30,000,000
7	Arrangement Fee Spread	0.5%-1%
8	Minimum Length of Lease Required	N/A
9	Usual Length of Loan	5-10 years
10	Investment	Yes
11	Refinance	Yes
12	Owner Occupier	Yes
13	Residential Investment	No
14	Development Finance	Yes
15	Residential Development	No
16	Hotels and Leisure	No
17	Healthcare	No
18	Bridging and/or Mezzanine Finance	No

Remarks

Investment property finance. Will consider both pre-let and speculative development for qualified borrowers (i.e. with a proven track record and business plan). Residential development will be considered when part of a mixed use scheme.

Kent Reliance Building Society

Reliance House
Manor Road
Chatham
Kent
ME4 6AF

Tel 01634 848944

Fax 01634 830912

Contact

Rob Procter

Criteria

1	Maximum Loan to Value	65% full commercial 75% residential investment let
2	Benchmark Lending Rate	7.2% variable base rate 9.2% variable minimum commercial rate 8.2% residential investment let rate
3	Margin Spread	2%-3%
4	Fixed	No
5	Minimum Loan	£25,000
6	Maximum Loan	£250,000
7	Arrangement Fee Spread	0.5% of advance minimum £250
8	Minimum Length of Lease Required	Term of loan plus 70 years
9	Usual Length of Loan	5-25 years
10	Investment	Yes
11	Refinance	Yes
12	Owner Occupier	Yes
13	Residential Investment	Yes
14	Development Finance	No
15	Residential Development	No
16	Hotels and Leisure	Yes
17	Healthcare	No
18	Bridging and/or Mezzanine Finance	No

Lambeth Building Society

118–120 Westminster Bridge Road
London
SE1 7XE

Tel 020 7928 1331

Fax 020 7261 0193

Contact

Gail Jackson

Criteria

1	Maximum Loan to Value	75%
2	Benchmark Lending Rate	Base
3	Margin Spread	1%-2%
4	Fixed	Yes
5	Minimum Loan	£15,001
6	Maximum Loan	£250,000
7	Arrangement Fee Spread	1%
8	Minimum Length of Lease Required	N/A
9	Usual Length of Loan	5-20 years
10	Investment	Yes
11	Refinance	Yes
12	Owner Occupier	Yes
13	Residential Investment	Yes
14	Development Finance	No
15	Residential Development	Yes
16	Hotels and Leisure	Yes
17	Healthcare	Yes
18	Bridging and/or Mezzanine Finance	No

Landesbank Hessen-Thüringen (Helaba)

11 Ironmonger Lane
London
EC2V 8JN

Tel 020 7334 4500/4556

Fax 020 7334 4502

Email: propertyfinance.uk@helaba.de

Contact

Peter Wilson
Graham Chapman
Chris Allsop
David Foord

Criteria

1	Maximum Loan to Value	80%
2	Benchmark Lending Rate	Libor
3	Margin Spread	1%-1.75% (higher on development loans)
4	Fixed	10 years available
5	Minimum Loan	£5,000,000
6	Maximum Loan	None
7	Arrangement Fee Spread	0.35%-0.80%
8	Minimum Length of Lease Required	None
9	Usual Length of Loan	3-15 years
10	Investment	Up to 15 years
11	Refinance	Yes
12	Owner Occupier	No
13	Residential Investment	No
14	Development Finance	Speculative: up to 60% of cost Pre-let: up to 90% of cost
15	Residential Development	No
16	Hotels and Leisure	No
17	Healthcare	No
18	Bridging and/or Mezzanine Finance	No

Remarks

Portfolio finance a speciality.

Leek United Building Society

50 St Edward Street
Leek
Staffordshire
ST13 5DH

Tel 01538 384151

Fax 01538 399179

Contact

Ruth Taylor

Criteria

1	Maximum Loan to Value	70%
2	Benchmark Lending Rate	N/A
3	Margin Spread	1%-2.5%
4	Fixed	Yes
5	Minimum Loan	£2,500
6	Maximum Loan	£300,000
7	Arrangement Fee Spread	1%
8	Minimum Length of Lease Required	N/A
9	Usual Length of Loan	5-20 years
10	Investment	Yes
11	Refinance	Yes
12	Owner Occupier	Yes
13	Residential Investment	Yes
14	Development Finance	No
15	Residential Development	Yes
16	Hotels and Leisure	Yes
17	Healthcare	No
18	Bridging and/or Mezzanine Finance	No

Remarks

Regional lender prefers within 60-mile radius of Leek.

Legal & General Bank

Temple Court
11 Queen Victoria Street
London EC4N 4TP

Tel 0800 096 6959

Contact

Peter Sanders

Criteria

1	Maximum Loan to Value	80%
2	Benchmark Lending Rate	3 month Libor
3	Margin Spread	1%-2%
4	Fixed	Yes, up to 30 years
5	Minimum Loan	£1,000,000
6	Maximum Loan	None
7	Arrangement Fee Spread	0.25%-1%
8	Minimum Length of Lease Required	70 years
9	Usual Length of Loan	10-25 years
10	Investment	Yes
11	Refinance	Yes
12	Owner Occupier	Yes
13	Residential Investment	No
14	Development Finance	No
15	Residential Development	No
16	Hotels and Leisure	No
17	Healthcare	No
18	Bridging and/or Mezzanine Finance	No

Leopold Joseph & Sons Ltd

99 Gresham Street
London
EC2V 7NG

Tel 020 7776 6700

Fax 020 7776 6740

Contact

Paul Thrussell

Criteria

1	Maximum Loan to Value	70%
2	Benchmark Lending Rate	Bank base
3	Margin Spread	1.5%-2.5%
4	Fixed	Yes, 5 years
5	Minimum Loan	£250,000
6	Maximum Loan	£5,000,000
7	Arrangement Fee Spread	0.5%-1%
8	Minimum Length of Lease Required	40 years
9	Usual Length of Loan	1-5 years
10	Investment	Yes
11	Refinance	Yes
12	Owner Occupier	Yes
13	Residential Investment	Yes
14	Development Finance	Yes
15	Residential Development	Yes
16	Hotels and Leisure	No
17	Healthcare	No
18	Bridging and/or Mezzanine Finance	No

Liverpool & Victoria

County Gates House
300 Poole Road
Bournemouth
Dorset
BH1 3NQ

Tel 01202 295544

Fax 01202 558712

Criteria

1	Maximum Loan to Value	70%
2	Benchmark Lending Rate	Libor
3	Margin Spread	Varies
4	Fixed	No
5	Minimum Loan	£25,000
6	Maximum Loan	£500,000
7	Arrangement Fee Spread	Varies
8	Minimum Length of Lease Required	None
9	Usual Length of Loan	1 - 10 years
10	Investment	Yes
11	Refinance	Yes
12	Owner Occupier	No
13	Residential Investment	No
14	Development Finance	No
15	Residential Development	No
16	Hotels and Leisure	No
17	Healthcare	No
18	Bridging and/or Mezzanine Finance	No

Lloyds TSB

Business Banking UKRB
PO Box 112
Canons House
Canons Way
Bristol
BS99 7LB

Tel 0117 943 3400

Fax 0117 943 3990

Contact

J M Whitaker
John Spence

Criteria

1	Maximum Loan to Value	Varies
2	Benchmark Lending Rate	Bank base/Libor/ Cost of funds
3	Margin Spread	1%–4.5%
4	Fixed	5–15 years
5	Minimum Loan	£1,000
6	Maximum Loan	£5,000,000
7	Arrangement Fee Spread	Negotiable
8	Minimum Length of Lease Required	Varies
9	Usual Length of Loan	1–25 years
10	Investment	Yes
11	Refinance	Yes
12	Owner Occupier	Yes
13	Residential Investment	Yes
14	Development Finance	Yes, pre-let
15	Residential Development	No
16	Hotels and Leisure	No
17	Healthcare	Yes
18	Bridging and/or Mezzanine Finance	No

Manchester Building Society

Queens Court
24 Queen Street
Manchester
M2 5AH

Tel 0161 833 8888

Fax 0161 833 8889

Contact

David Cowie

Criteria

1	Maximum Loan to Value	85%
2	Benchmark Lending Rate	Standard variable rate
3	Margin Spread	Varies
4	Fixed	Yes
5	Minimum Loan	£50,000
6	Maximum Loan	£1,000,000
7	Arrangement Fee Spread	0.5%-1.5%
8	Minimum Length of Lease Required	40 years
9	Usual Length of Loan	5-30 years
10	Investment	Yes
11	Refinance	Yes
12	Owner Occupier	Yes
13	Residential Investment	Yes
14	Development Finance	No
15	Residential Development	Yes
16	Hotels and Leisure	Yes
17	Healthcare	Yes
18	Bridging and/or Mezzanine Finance	Yes

Remarks

Prefers to lend within 50-mile radius of Manchester.

W M Mann & Co (Investments) Ltd

201 Bath Street
Glasgow
G2 4HY

Tel 0141 248 4936

Fax 0141 221 2976

Email: mann@201bathstreet.fsnet.co.uk

Contact

Bruce Mann, Director
Alan McKinlay, Director

Criteria

1	Maximum Loan to Value	70%
2	Benchmark Lending Rate	Clydesdale Bank base
3	Margin Spread	3.5%-4.5%
4	Fixed	No
5	Minimum Loan	£25,500
6	Maximum Loan	£425,000
7	Arrangement Fee Spread	1%-2%
8	Minimum Length of Lease Required	Freehold only
9	Usual Length of Loan	6 months-15 years
10	Investment	Yes
11	Refinance	Occasionally
12	Owner Occupier	Yes
13	Residential Investment	Yes
14	Development Finance	Yes
15	Residential Development	Yes
16	Hotels and Leisure	Yes
17	Healthcare	Yes
18	Bridging and/or Mezzanine Finance	Yes

Remarks

Commercial lending only in Scotland, especially residential and retail development.

Mansfield Building Society

Regent House
Regent Street
Mansfield
Nottinghamshire
NG18 1SS

Tel 01623 676300

Fax 01623 420261

Email: enquiries@mansfieldbs.co.uk

Contact

S Hughes

Criteria

1	Maximum Loan to Value	75%
2	Benchmark Lending Rate	Standard variable rate
3	Margin Spread	+1% subject to assessment of the proposition
4	Fixed	No
5	Minimum Loan	£25,001
6	Maximum Loan	£500,000
7	Arrangement Fee Spread	1%
8	Minimum Length of Lease Required	N/A
9	Usual Length of Loan	15 years
10	Investment	Yes
11	Refinance	Yes
12	Owner Occupier	Yes
13	Residential Investment	Yes
14	Development Finance	No
15	Residential Development	Yes
16	Hotels and Leisure	Yes
17	Healthcare	No
18	Bridging and/or Mezzanine Finance	No

Marsden Building Society

6-20 Russell Street
Nelson
Lancashire
BB9 7NJ

Tel 01282 440500

Fax 01282 440 550

Contact

Martin Mulligan

Criteria

1	Maximum Loan to Value	75%
2	Benchmark Lending Rate	Standard variable rate
3	Margin Spread	1%–1.25%
4	Fixed	Yes
5	Minimum Loan	£15,000
6	Maximum Loan	£500,000
7	Arrangement Fee Spread	1%
8	Minimum Length of Lease Required	N/A
9	Usual Length of Loan	10–25 years
10	Investment	Yes
11	Refinance	Yes
12	Owner Occupier	Yes
13	Residential Investment	Yes
14	Development Finance	No
15	Residential Development	No
16	Hotels and Leisure	Yes
17	Healthcare	No
18	Bridging and/or Mezzanine Finance	No

Remarks

Regional lending only. 100-mile radius of Marsden.

Mercantile Building Society

Mercantile House
The Silverlink Business Park
Wallsend
Tyne & Wear
NE28 9NY

Tel 0191 295 9500

Fax 0191 262 6026

Contact

Jill Lloyd

Criteria

1	Maximum Loan to Value	75%
2	Benchmark Lending Rate	Variable base rate
3	Margin Spread	Up to 2%
4	Fixed	Will consider
5	Minimum Loan	£15,000
6	Maximum Loan	£500,000
7	Arrangement Fee Spread	1%
8	Minimum Length of Lease Required	60 years
9	Usual Length of Loan	10-20 years
10	Investment	Yes
11	Refinance	Yes
12	Owner Occupier	Yes
13	Residential Investment	Yes
14	Development Finance	Yes
15	Residential Development	Yes
16	Hotels and Leisure	No
17	Healthcare	No
18	Bridging and/or Mezzanine Finance	No

Merrill Lynch International Ltd

European Real Estate Group
25 Ropemaker Street
London
EC2Y 9LY

Tel 020 7995 2787/2814/4581/2000

Fax 020 7867 2008

Contact

Naji E Boutros

Criteria

1	Maximum Loan to Value	100%
2	Benchmark Lending Rate	Varies
3	Margin Spread	Varies
4	Fixed	No
5	Minimum Loan	£20,000,000
6	Maximum Loan	None
7	Arrangement Fee Spread	Varies
8	Minimum Length of Lease Required	N/A
9	Usual Length of Loan	Varies
10	Investment	Yes
11	Refinance	Yes
12	Owner Occupier	Not usually
13	Residential Investment	In exceptional circumstances
14	Development Finance	Yes, pre-let only
15	Residential Development	Rarely
16	Hotels and Leisure	Yes
17	Healthcare	Yes
18	Bridging and/or Mezzanine Finance	Yes

Remarks

Lends only to larger Plcs and major property players. Will lend or arrange loans worldwide.
Prefers to lend on large portfolios, including leisure. Large refinancing of existing holdings also possible.

Midland Bank

Contact

Contact the commercial mortgage manager at the nearest branch to the property concerned. To obtain the branch address and number call:
020 7260 8000

Criteria

1	Maximum Loan to Value	Varies
2	Benchmark Lending Rate	Bank base/Libor/ Cost of funds
3	Margin Spread	1%-4.5%
4	Fixed	5-15 years
5	Minimum Loan	£1,000
6	Maximum Loan	None
7	Arrangement Fee Spread	Negotiable
8	Minimum Length of Lease Required	Varies
9	Usual Length of Loan	1-25 years
10	Investment	Yes
11	Refinance	Yes
12	Owner Occupier	Yes
13	Residential Investment	Yes
14	Development Finance	Yes, pre-let
15	Residential Development	No
16	Hotels and Leisure	Yes
17	Healthcare	Yes
18	Bridging and/or Mezzanine Finance	No

J P Morgan & Co

60 Wall Street
New York
New York 10260-0060
USA

Tel 001 212 483 2323

Contact

Jacques Thunnissen
(New York)
Managing Director
Michael Barbour
Head of Operations

Criteria

1	Maximum Loan to Value	95%
2	Benchmark Lending Rate	Cost of funds
3	Margin Spread	Varies
4	Fixed	Yes
5	Minimum Loan	£15,000,000
6	Maximum Loan	None
7	Arrangement Fee Spread	Varies
8	Minimum Length of Lease Required	N/A
9	Usual Length of Loan	25 years
10	Investment	Yes
11	Refinance	Yes
12	Owner Occupier	Yes
13	Residential Investment	Yes
14	Development Finance	Yes
15	Residential Development	Yes
16	Hotels and Leisure	Yes
17	Healthcare	Yes
18	Bridging and/or Mezzanine Finance	Yes

Remarks

Lends to major property companies and established investors and developers.

Morgan Guaranty Trust Co (J P Morgan)

60 Victoria Embankment
London
EC4Y 0JP

Tel 020 7600 2300

Fax 020 7325 5906

Contact

Linda Fussell
Mark Danzel

Criteria

1	Maximum Loan to Value	Variable
2	Benchmark Lending Rate	Base
3	Margin Spread	Negotiable
4	Fixed	No
5	Minimum Loan	£20,000,000
6	Maximum Loan	None
7	Arrangement Fee Spread	Variable
8	Minimum Length of Lease Required	None
9	Usual Length of Loan	1 – 10 years
10	Investment	Sometimes
11	Refinance	Sometimes
12	Owner Occupier	No
13	Residential Investment	No
14	Development Finance	No
15	Residential Development	No
16	Hotels and Leisure	Yes
17	Healthcare	Yes
18	Bridging and/or Mezzanine Finance	Yes

Remarks

Primarily funding for hotel and leisure industry.

Morgan Stanley Dean Witter

25 Cabot Square
Canary Wharf
London
E14 1QA

Tel 020 7425 5654

Fax 020 7425 3834

Email: john.carrafiell@morganstanley.com

Contact

John A. Carrafiell – Managing Director, Head of European Real Estate
Lynn Maclean – Executive Director, Head of European Lending

Criteria

1	Maximum Loan to Value	85%
2	Benchmark Lending Rate	Fixed rate
3	Margin Spread	1%-1.9%
4	Fixed	Yes - for term of loan
5	Minimum Loan	£1,000,000
6	Maximum Loan	£500,000,000
7	Arrangement Fee Spread	0.5%
8	Minimum Length of Lease Required	N/A
9	Usual Length of Loan	Max. 7 years
10	Investment	Yes
11	Refinance	Yes
12	Owner Occupier	Yes
13	Residential Investment	Yes
14	Development Finance	No
15	Residential Development	No
16	Hotels and Leisure	Yes
17	Healthcare	No
18	Bridging and/or Mezzanine Finance	No

Remarks

36 hours credit approval from agreement of terms.

National Counties Building Society

National Counties House
Church Street
Epsom
Surrey
KT19 4NL

Tel 01372 742 211

Fax 01372 745 607

Contact

Stewart Glover –
Manager special
schemes and
agreements

Criteria

1	Maximum Loan to Value	70%
2	Benchmark Lending Rate	Society's base rate
3	Margin Spread	1%-3%
4	Fixed	No
5	Minimum Loan	£50,000 (£30,000 residential investment)
6	Maximum Loan	£5,000,000 company
7	Arrangement Fee Spread	£200 min to 1%, plus valuation £2.50 per £1000
8	Minimum Length of Lease Required	50 years at end of mortgage
9	Usual Length of Loan	5-25 years
10	Investment	Yes
11	Refinance	Yes
12	Owner Occupier	Yes
13	Residential Investment	Yes
14	Development Finance	No
15	Residential Development	No
16	Hotels and Leisure	Yes
17	Healthcare	Yes
18	Bridging and/or Mezzanine Finance	No

Remarks

Varied but do not consider care and retirement homes. Agricultural limited to 50% investment value and Public Houses limited to 50%. Minimum valuation £2,000,000. Commercial residential investment £55,000 flats, £80,000 houses. Residential investment criteria available upon request. In principle decision within 48 hours. Maximum LTV dependent on security.

National Westminster Bank Plc

Structured Finance
Property Finance Group
5th Floor
No 1 Princes Street
London
EC2R 8PB

Tel 020 7390 1213

Fax 020 7390 1767

Email: stephen.eighteen@cbs.natwest.com

Contact

Stephen Eighteen

Criteria

1	Maximum Loan to Value	Varies
2	Benchmark Lending Rate	Libor/Cost of funds/Base
3	Margin Spread	Varies
4	Fixed	5-25 years
5	Minimum Loan	£10,000,000
6	Maximum Loan	None
7	Arrangement Fee Spread	Negotiable
8	Minimum Length of Lease Required	None
9	Usual Length of Loan	1-25 years
10	Investment	Yes
11	Refinance	Yes
12	Owner Occupier	Yes
13	Residential Investment	Yes
14	Development Finance	Pre-let only
15	Residential Development	No
16	Hotels and Leisure	Yes
17	Healthcare	No
18	Bridging and/or Mezzanine Finance	Yes - sometimes

Nationwide Building Society

Business Finance
Kings Park Road
Moulton Park
Northampton
NN3 6NW

Tel 08457 023740

Fax 01604 793278

Contact

Linda Mansfield

Criteria

1	Maximum Loan to Value	70%
2	Benchmark Lending Rate	Libor
3	Margin Spread	Libor 2.5%-3.5%
4	Fixed	Yes
5	Minimum Loan	£50,000
6	Maximum Loan	None
7	Arrangement Fee Spread	1%
8	Minimum Length of Lease Required	30 years remaining at end of mortgage
9	Usual Length of Loan	5-25 years
10	Investment	Yes
11	Refinance	Yes
12	Owner Occupier	Yes
13	Residential Investment	Yes
14	Development Finance	No
15	Residential Development	No
16	Hotels and Leisure	No
17	Healthcare	No
18	Bridging and/or Mezzanine Finance	No

Remarks

Key lending sectors are investment property and professionals.
No start-ups.

Newbury Building Society

17–20 Bartholomew Street
Newbury
Berkshire
RG14 5LY

Tel 01635 555700

Fax 01635 555799

Email: mail@newbury.co.uk

Contact

Phillippa Cardno

Criteria

1	Maximum Loan to Value	75%
2	Benchmark Lending Rate	Lender base (6.11% currently)
3	Margin Spread	0.5%-2%
4	Fixed	No
5	Minimum Loan	£30,000
6	Maximum Loan	£750,000
7	Arrangement Fee Spread	0.25%-1%
8	Minimum Length of Lease Required	30 years plus length of loan
9	Usual Length of Loan	5-20 years
10	Investment	Yes
11	Refinance	Yes
12	Owner Occupier	Yes
13	Residential Investment	Yes
14	Development Finance	No
15	Residential Development	No
16	Hotels and Leisure	Yes
17	Healthcare	Yes
18	Bridging and/or Mezzanine Finance	No

Remarks

All types of quality property funded within 60-mile radius of Newbury.

Newcastle Building Society

Portland House
New Bridge Street
Newcastle-upon-Tyne
NE1 8AL

Tel 0191 244 2295/2256/2243

Fax 0191 244 2271

Contact

Jayne Dickens
David Widdowson
David Nelson

Criteria

1	Maximum Loan to Value	85%
2	Benchmark Lending Rate	Building society base/ Libor/Fixed rates
3	Margin Spread	0%-2%
4	Fixed	Yes
5	Minimum Loan	£50,000
6	Maximum Loan	£10,000,000
7	Arrangement Fee Spread	0.25%-1%
8	Minimum Length of Lease Required	60 years
9	Usual Length of Loan	5-25 years
10	Investment	Yes
11	Refinance	Yes
12	Owner Occupier	Yes
13	Residential Investment	Yes
14	Development Finance	No
15	Residential Development	No
16	Hotels and Leisure	No
17	Healthcare	No
18	Bridging and/or Mezzanine Finance	No

Remarks

Individual facilities tailored to meet borrowers' specific requirements. Key values of personal service and flexibility.

Nomura Bank International

Nomura House
1 St Martin Le Grand
London
EC1A 4NP

Tel 020 7696 6871/7521 3857

Fax 020 7248 5497/7236 7711

Contact

J G S Macdonald
Charles Bowen
Guy Hands
Douglas Grant
James Turner

Criteria

1	Maximum Loan to Value	80%
2	Benchmark Lending Rate	3 month Libor
3	Margin Spread	0.90%-1.75%
4	Fixed	Yes
5	Minimum Loan	£5,000,000
6	Maximum Loan	None
7	Arrangement Fee Spread	0.25%-1%
8	Minimum Length of Lease Required	Varies
9	Usual Length of Loan	Up to 5 years
10	Investment	Yes
11	Refinance	Yes
12	Owner Occupier	Yes
13	Residential Investment	No
14	Development Finance	No
15	Residential Development	No
16	Hotels and Leisure	No
17	Healthcare	No
18	Bridging and/or Mezzanine Finance	Yes

Remarks

Lends almost exclusively to major Plcs and property companies.

Nordea

19 Thomas More Street
London
E1W 1YF

Tel 020 7265 3333

Fax 020 7265 3237

Email: william.goldstein@nordea.com

Contact

William Goldstein
Tel: 020 7265 3300
Steve Ambridge
Tel: 020 7265 3299

Criteria

1	Maximum Loan to Value	80%
2	Benchmark Lending Rate	Bank base/3 month Libor
3	Margin Spread	1%-2%
4	Fixed	Yes
5	Minimum Loan	£500,000
6	Maximum Loan	£20,000,000
7	Arrangement Fee Spread	0.25%-1%
8	Minimum Length of Lease Required	Loan period plus 5 years
9	Usual Length of Loan	Up to 10 years
10	Investment	Yes
11	Refinance	Yes
12	Owner Occupier	Only for clients of first-class financial standing
13	Residential Investment	As part of mixed portfolio
14	Development Finance	Yes, with pre-let
15	Residential Development	No
16	Hotels and Leisure	Yes subject to operator's lease
17	Healthcare	No
18	Bridging and/or Mezzanine Finance	No

Remarks

Formerly Merita Nordbanken.

Northern Bank Ltd

Donegal Square West
Belfast
BT1 EJS

Tel 01232 245 277

Fax 01232 893 337

Contact

Winston Fletcher
Ext 3651

Criteria

1	Maximum Loan to Value	75%
2	Benchmark Lending Rate	Base
3	Margin Spread	1%-2%
4	Fixed	No
5	Minimum Loan	£15,000
6	Maximum Loan	None
7	Arrangement Fee Spread	0.25%-1%
8	Minimum Length of Lease Required	None
9	Usual Length of Loan	1 month-30 years
10	Investment	Yes
11	Refinance	Yes
12	Owner Occupier	Yes
13	Residential Investment	Yes
14	Development Finance	Yes
15	Residential Development	Yes
16	Hotels and Leisure	Yes
17	Healthcare	Yes
18	Bridging and/or Mezzanine Finance	No

Remarks

Currently lending only in Northern Ireland. Will lend against all types of property, including hotels and leisure.

Northern Rock Plc

Head Office
Northern Rock Commercial Finance
Doxford International Business Park
Sunderland SR3 3XG

Contact

Fiona Young, Scotland
Tel: 0131 226 4715
or 0141 221 7886
Phillip Barker, Newcastle
Tel: 0191 221 0383
Alan Laslett, Leeds
Tel: 0113 243 9904
Sally Peverley,
Birmingham
Tel: 0121 643 5153
Tony Hart, Bristol
Tel: 0117 930 0575
Samantha Shillingford,
Manchester
Tel: 0161 834 6484
Nick Spittall, St Albans
Tel: 01727 837364
Alasdair Caie, Bromley
Tel: 020 8466 6816
Lisa Elverd, Reading
Tel: 0118 950 0349

Criteria

1	Maximum Loan to Value	75%
2	Benchmark Lending Rate	Building society variable base rate/3 month Libor/ Commercial tracker
3	Margin Spread	1.5%-2.5%
4	Fixed	Yes, subject to availability
5	Minimum Loan	£30,000 £100,000 offices, retail £250,000 nursing homes
6	Maximum Loan	£10,000,000 +
7	Arrangement Fee Spread	0.5%-1%
8	Minimum Length of Lease Required	Mortgage term plus 30 years
9	Usual Length of Loan	5-25 years
10	Investment	Yes
11	Refinance	Yes
12	Owner Occupier	Yes
13	Residential Investment	Yes
14	Development Finance	Pre-let/owner-occupied commercial developments considered
15	Residential Development	No
16	Hotels and Leisure	Yes
17	Healthcare	Yes
18	Bridging and/or Mezzanine Finance	No

Remarks

All lending secured against commercial property assets. Principal features being speed of decision making, practical and flexible approach, with an emphasis that is very much relationship orientated.

Norwich & Peterborough Building Society

Chief Office
Peterborough Business Park
Lynch Wood
Peterborough
PE2 6WZ

Tel 01733 372425

Fax 01733 372229

Email: stuart.benge@npbs.co.uk

Contact

Stuart Benge
Tel: 01733 372242

Criteria

1	Maximum Loan to Value	75% (80% on new, owner occupied industrial units)
2	Benchmark Lending Rate	Libor/Mortgage base
3	Margin Spread	0.5%-3% (Libor) 0%-2% (base)
4	Fixed	Available - please enquire
5	Minimum Loan	£30,000
6	Maximum Loan	£5,000,000
7	Arrangement Fee Spread	0.5%-1%
8	Minimum Length of Lease Required	50 years at the end of loan on long leasehold
9	Usual Length of Loan	5-25 years
10	Investment	Yes
11	Refinance	Yes
12	Owner Occupier	Yes
13	Residential Investment	No
14	Development Finance	No
15	Residential Development	No
16	Hotels and Leisure	Yes
17	Healthcare	Yes
18	Bridging and/or Mezzanine Finance	No

Remarks

Industrial units, offices, shops, sub-post offices, commercial investment properties, nursing/residential care homes, guest houses, small hotels, professional loans, public houses, private schools, self-administered and self-invested pension scheme loans and housing associations.
Charges a higher advance fee where an advance exceeds 75% of valuation or purchase price, whichever is the lower.

Norwich Union Plc

Norwich Union Mortgage Finance
P.O. Box 21
Surrey Street
Norwich
NR1 3NJ

Tel 01603 682276/685619

Fax 01603 878685

Contact

Jayne Benton

Criteria

1	Maximum Loan to Value	80%
2	Benchmark Lending Rate	Gilts
3	Margin Spread	1.6%-2.0%
4	Fixed	Yes
5	Minimum Loan	£1,000,000
6	Maximum Loan	None
7	Arrangement Fee Spread	0.15% of the loan amount
8	Minimum Length of Lease Required	At least 35 years unexpired at the end of the mortgage term
9	Usual Length of Loan	5-25 years
10	Investment	Yes
11	Refinance	Yes
12	Owner Occupier	No
13	Residential Investment	No
14	Development Finance	No
15	Residential Development	No
16	Hotels and Leisure	No
17	Healthcare	No
18	Bridging and/or Mezzanine Finance	No

P L T Ltd

Third Floor
29–30 Cornhill
London
EC3V 3ND

Tel 020 7256 3411

Fax 020 7256 3401

Contact

Matthew Rayer-Kennedy
Jeremy Robinson

Criteria

1	Maximum Loan to Value	65%
2	Benchmark Lending Rate	Finance house base rate
3	Margin Spread	3%-5%
4	Fixed	No
5	Minimum Loan	£250,000
6	Maximum Loan	£3,000,000
7	Arrangement Fee Spread	1%
8	Minimum Length of Lease Required	N/A
9	Usual Length of Loan	c. 12 months
10	Investment	No
11	Refinance	Yes, if residential development ensues
12	Owner Occupier	No
13	Residential Investment	No
14	Development Finance	Residential only
15	Residential Development	Yes
16	Hotels and Leisure	No
17	Healthcare	No
18	Bridging and/or Mezzanine Finance	No

Remarks

Specialists in Residential Development finance for new build, conversion or renovation.

Portman Building Society

40 Portman Square
London
W1H 9FH

Tel 020 7935 0981

Fax 020 7224 4183

Contact

Roger Behagg

Criteria

1	Maximum Loan to Value	80%, but up to 85% of cost
2	Benchmark Lending Rate	3 months Libor, swap market
3	Margin Spread	0.9%-1.25%
4	Fixed	Up to 10 years
5	Minimum Loan	£500,000
6	Maximum Loan	£40,000,000
7	Arrangement Fee Spread	0.25%-0.5%
8	Minimum Length of Lease Required	Unless amortising - 13 years
9	Usual Length of Loan	3-30 years
10	Investment	Yes
11	Refinance	Yes
12	Owner Occupier	Yes
13	Residential Investment	Yes
14	Development Finance	No
15	Residential Development	Yes
16	Hotels and Leisure	No
17	Healthcare	No
18	Bridging and/or Mezzanine Finance	No

Remarks

Currently lending restricted to Central London only.

Principality Building Society

Principality Buildings
Queen Street
Cardiff
CF1 1UA

Tel 02920 44188

Fax 01222 374567

Contact

James Jamieson
Michael McGuire

Criteria

1	Maximum Loan to Value	75%
2	Benchmark Lending Rate	Standard variable rate
3	Margin Spread	Up to 2%
4	Fixed	Residential only
5	Minimum Loan	£15,000
6	Maximum Loan	£500,000
7	Arrangement Fee Spread	0.75%-1.25%
8	Minimum Length of Lease Required	30 years
9	Usual Length of Loan	5-25 years
10	Investment	Yes
11	Refinance	Yes
12	Owner Occupier	Yes
13	Residential Investment	Yes
14	Development Finance	Yes
15	Residential Development	Yes
16	Hotels and Leisure	No
17	Healthcare	No
18	Bridging and/or Mezzanine Finance	No

Remarks

Lending in Wales only.

Property Mezzanine Partners

1st Floor
Sloane Square House
Holbein Place
London SW1W 8NS

Tel 020 7730 8330

Fax 020 7730 9323

Contact

Graham Morris

Criteria

1	Maximum Loan to Value	Mezzanine finance only up to 95%
2	Benchmark Lending Rate	Libor
3	Margin Spread	Variable
4	Fixed	Yes
5	Minimum Loan	£500,000
6	Maximum Loan	£4,000,000+
7	Arrangement Fee Spread	Variable
8	Minimum Length of Lease Required	None
9	Usual Length of Loan	Up to 3 years
10	Investment	Yes
11	Refinance	Yes
12	Owner Occupier	Yes
13	Residential Investment	Central London only
14	Development Finance	Pre-let only
15	Residential Development	Central London only
16	Hotels and Leisure	Sometimes
17	Healthcare	No
18	Bridging and/or Mezzanine Finance	Yes

Remarks

All proposals must be accompanied by a business plan.

Prudential Portfolio Managers Ltd

142 Holborn Bars
London
EC1N 2NH

Tel 020 7548 3089/3936
020 7548 3145

Fax 020 7548 3989

Contact

Steven Chamberlain
Dennis Collins
Martin Walsh

Criteria

1	Maximum Loan to Value	85%
2	Benchmark Lending Rate	3 month Libor/relevant Gilt
3	Margin Spread	1%-2%
4	Fixed	Yes, up to 30 years
5	Minimum Loan	£1,000,000
6	Maximum Loan	None
7	Arrangement Fee Spread	0.25%-0.5%
8	Minimum Length of Lease Required	70 years
9	Usual Length of Loan	15-30 years
10	Investment	Yes
11	Refinance	Yes
12	Owner Occupier	Yes
13	Residential Investment	No
14	Development Finance	No
15	Residential Development	No
16	Hotels and Leisure	Yes
17	Healthcare	Yes
18	Bridging and/or Mezzanine Finance	No

Remarks

Specialises in lending long term on fixed rate on all types of UK quality commercial property.

Regentsmead Ltd

Russell House
140 High Street
Edgware
Middlesex
HA8 7LW

Tel 020 8952 1414

Fax 020 8952 2424

Email: jbloom@regentsmead.com

Contact

James Bloom, Director

Criteria

1	Maximum Loan to Value	65% (up to 100% of development costs)
2	Benchmark Lending Rate	1.25% per month
3	Margin Spread	1%–1.5% per month
4	Fixed	Yes
5	Minimum Loan	£50,000
6	Maximum Loan	£2,000,000
7	Arrangement Fee Spread	None
8	Minimum Length of Lease Required	90 years
9	Usual Length of Loan	Up to 12 months
10	Investment	Yes
11	Refinance	Yes
12	Owner Occupier	Yes
13	Residential Investment	Yes
14	Development Finance	Yes
15	Residential Development	Yes
16	Hotels and Leisure	Yes
17	Healthcare	No
18	Bridging and/or Mezzanine Finance	Yes

Remarks

Very keen on quality development finance but will look at all short-term funding required. Aims to issue offer in principle within 24 hours of receiving suitable proposal.

Republic National Bank of New York

47 Berkeley Square
London
W1X 5DB

Tel 020 7860 3000/3175

Fax 020 7860 3028
020 7629 4015

Contact

Brian Andrews

Criteria

1	Maximum Loan to Value	65%
2	Benchmark Lending Rate	Bank base
3	Margin Spread	Varies
4	Fixed	Yes
5	Minimum Loan	£500,000
6	Maximum Loan	£5,000,000
7	Arrangement Fee Spread	1%
8	Minimum Length of Lease Required	Freehold only
9	Usual Length of Loan	Varies
10	Investment	For existing clients only
11	Refinance	No
12	Owner Occupier	No
13	Residential Investment	Yes
14	Development Finance	Yes, residential only
15	Residential Development	Yes
16	Hotels and Leisure	No
17	Healthcare	No
18	Bridging and/or Mezzanine Finance	No

Remarks

Currently only carrying out preliminary lending on residential properties and investments.

Rheinische Hypothekenbank AG

Taunustor 3
60311 Frankfurt am Main
Germany

London Representative Office
55 Bishopsgate
London
EC2N 3AS

Tel 00 49 69 23 82 347
Fax 00 49 69 23 82 5000

Tel 020 7638 5400
Fax 020 7638 5152

Contact

Anni Hönicke
G Fiordelisi
Mark Titcomb (UK)
Christopher Hunter (UK)

Criteria

1	Maximum Loan to Value	90%
2	Benchmark Lending Rate	Cost of funds
3	Margin Spread	0.6%-1.5%
4	Fixed	Yes
5	Minimum Loan	£4,000,000
6	Maximum Loan	None
7	Arrangement Fee Spread	0.25%
8	Minimum Length of Lease Required	60 years plus length of loan
9	Usual Length of Loan	3-15 years
10	Investment	Yes
11	Refinance	Yes
12	Owner Occupier	Only for clients of first-class financial standing
13	Residential Investment	No
14	Development Finance	No
15	Residential Development	No
16	Hotels and Leisure	No
17	Healthcare	No
18	Bridging and/or Mezzanine Finance	No

Remarks

Lends to most EU countries.

Riggs Bank Europe Ltd

21 Great Winchester Street
London
EC2N 2HH

Tel 020 7588 7575 (switchboard)

Fax 020 7374 2629

Email: david.catherall@riggsbank.co.uk

Contact

David A Catherall
Tel: 020 7614 4330

Criteria

1	Maximum Loan to Value	75% lower of cost or valuation
2	Benchmark Lending Rate	Libor
3	Margin Spread	1.25% +
4	Fixed	Up to 5 years
5	Minimum Loan	£500,000
6	Maximum Loan	£10,000,000
7	Arrangement Fee Spread	Up to 1%
8	Minimum Length of Lease Required	None
9	Usual Length of Loan	5 years
10	Investment	Yes
11	Refinance	Yes, provided minimum cash-out
12	Owner Occupier	No
13	Residential Investment	Yes
14	Development Finance	Yes – pre-let/pre-sold
15	Residential Development	Yes – smaller schemes
16	Hotels and Leisure	Yes – dependent on lease terms and covenants
17	Healthcare	Yes – dependent on lease terms and covenants
18	Bridging and/or Mezzanine Finance	No

N M Rothschild & Sons

New Court
St Swithin's Lane
London
EC4P 4DU

Tel 020 7280 5745

Fax 020 7280 5504

Contact

Andrew Radkiewicz – Head of Property Finance
Tel: 020 7280 5745
Claire Livingstone – Manager
Tel: 020 7280 5743

Criteria

1	Maximum Loan to Value	90%
2	Benchmark Lending Rate	Libor
3	Margin Spread	1%-2%
4	Fixed	Yes
5	Minimum Loan	£2,000,000
6	Maximum Loan	None
7	Arrangement Fee Spread	0.25%-1.0%
8	Minimum Length of Lease Required	No
9	Usual Length of Loan	5 years
10	Investment	Yes
11	Refinance	Yes
12	Owner Occupier	No
13	Residential Investment	Yes
14	Development Finance	Yes
15	Residential Development	Yes
16	Hotels and Leisure	No
17	Healthcare	No
18	Bridging and/or Mezzanine Finance	No

The Royal Bank of Scotland Plc

Structured Property Finance
Level 5
135 Bishopsgate
London EC2M 3UR

Tel 020 7648 3944

Fax 020 7648 3524

Email: paul.aubery@rbs.co.uk

Contact

Paul Aubery,
Associate Director
Tel: 020 7648 3940
Christian Mathews,
Associate Director
Tel: 020 7648 3944

Criteria

1	Maximum Loan to Value	Varies
2	Benchmark Lending Rate	Libor/Cost of funds/ Base rate
3	Margin Spread	Varies
4	Fixed	2-25 years
5	Minimum Loan	£10,000,000
6	Maximum Loan	None
7	Arrangement Fee Spread	Negotiable
8	Minimum Length of Lease Required	None
9	Usual Length of Loan	1-25 years
10	Investment	Yes
11	Refinance	Yes
12	Owner Occupier	Yes
13	Residential Investment	Yes
14	Development Finance	Yes - pre-let only
15	Residential Development	Yes
16	Hotels and Leisure	Yes
17	Healthcare	Yes
18	Bridging and/or Mezzanine Finance	No

Remarks

Active in providing a range of funding solutions including joint venture equity, mezzanine and senior debt.

Saffron Walden Herts & Essex Building Society

Market Street
Saffron Walden
Essex
CB10 1HX

Tel 01799 522211

Fax 01799 513622

Contact

Gillian Ashbridge

Criteria

1	Maximum Loan to Value	75%
2	Benchmark Lending Rate	8.25%
3	Margin Spread	1%-2.5%
4	Fixed	No
5	Minimum Loan	£10,000
6	Maximum Loan	£250,000
7	Arrangement Fee Spread	0%-1.5%
8	Minimum Length of Lease Required	50 years following term expiry
9	Usual Length of Loan	25 years
10	Investment	Yes
11	Refinance	Yes
12	Owner Occupier	Yes
13	Residential Investment	Yes
14	Development Finance	Yes
15	Residential Development	Yes
16	Hotels and Leisure	Yes
17	Healthcare	No
18	Bridging and/or Mezzanine Finance	No

Remarks

Prefers lending on residential investment and developments.

Sainsbury's Bank

City House
City Road
Chester
CH88 3YE

Tel 0800 096 0541

Contact

Derek Jamieson
Carol Chittonden

Criteria

1	Maximum Loan to Value	75%
2	Benchmark Lending Rate	Libor
3	Margin Spread	1%
4	Fixed	Yes
5	Minimum Loan	£25,001
6	Maximum Loan	£1,000,000
7	Arrangement Fee Spread	1%
8	Minimum Length of Lease Required	N/A
9	Usual Length of Loan	5-25 years
10	Investment	No
11	Refinance	No
12	Owner Occupier	No
13	Residential Investment	Yes
14	Development Finance	No
15	Residential Development	Yes
16	Hotels and Leisure	No
17	Healthcare	No
18	Bridging and/or Mezzanine Finance	No

Sanwa Bank

Citiplace House
55 Basinghall Street
London
EC2V 5DL

Tel 020 7330 5000

Fax 020 7330 5555

Contact

Stephen B Lewis

Criteria

1	Maximum Loan to Value	80%
2	Benchmark Lending Rate	3 month Libor
3	Margin Spread	1%-2%
4	Fixed	Yes
5	Minimum Loan	£3,000,000
6	Maximum Loan	None
7	Arrangement Fee Spread	0.25%-1%
8	Minimum Length of Lease Required	Varies
9	Usual Length of Loan	1-10 years
10	Investment	Yes
11	Refinance	Yes
12	Owner Occupier	Yes
13	Residential Investment	No
14	Development Finance	Pre-let only
15	Residential Development	No
16	Hotels and Leisure	No
17	Healthcare	No
18	Bridging and/or Mezzanine Finance	No

Remarks

Currently lending to existing clients only.

Scottish Agricultural Securities Corporation Plc

19 Rutland Square
Edinburgh
EH1 2BA

Tel 0141 223 2598

Fax 0131 220 2912

Contact

John Mirtle

Criteria

1	Maximum Loan to Value	66%
2	Benchmark Lending Rate	Cost of fixed rate funds
3	Margin Spread	Varies
4	Fixed	Yes
5	Minimum Loan	£15,001
6	Maximum Loan	£2,000,000
7	Arrangement Fee Spread	None
8	Minimum Length of Lease Required	Freehold only
9	Usual Length of Loan	5–25 years
10	Investment	No
11	Refinance	Yes
12	Owner Occupier	Yes
13	Residential Investment	No
14	Development Finance	No
15	Residential Development	No
16	Hotels and Leisure	No
17	Healthcare	No
18	Bridging and/or Mezzanine Finance	No

Remarks

Loans on agricultural properties only. Lending exclusively to existing clients only.

Singer & Friedlander

21 New Street
London
EC2M 4HR

Tel 020 7623 3000

Fax 020 7975 3688

Contact

Charles Mavor
David Penston

Criteria

1	Maximum Loan to Value	75%
2	Benchmark Lending Rate	3 month Libor
3	Margin Spread	1.75%-3.0%
4	Fixed	Sometimes
5	Minimum Loan	£1,000,000
6	Maximum Loan	£7,500,000
7	Arrangement Fee Spread	0.5%-1%
8	Minimum Length of Lease Required	70 years
9	Usual Length of Loan	1-2 years
10	Investment	Yes
11	Refinance	No
12	Owner Occupier	No
13	Residential Investment	Yes
14	Development Finance	Yes
15	Residential Development	Yes
16	Hotels and Leisure	Yes
17	Healthcare	Yes
18	Bridging and/or Mezzanine Finance	Yes

Remarks

Prefers to lend in the development sector - will also fund commercial refurbishment. Will look at residential development funding or refurbishment of office buildings, residential in large city centres only. No speculative commercial development finance.

100% development packages considered. Preferred size for these: £1m-£5m. Investment roll-up possible.

Société Générale

Exchange House
Primrose Street
Broadgate
London
EC2A 2HT

Tel 020 7762 4444

Fax 020 7638 7169

Contact

Etienne Thoreau

Criteria

1	Maximum Loan to Value	75%
2	Benchmark Lending Rate	3 month Libor
3	Margin Spread	0.85%-1.5%
4	Fixed	Yes
5	Minimum Loan	£5,000,000
6	Maximum Loan	None
7	Arrangement Fee Spread	0.25%-0.5%
8	Minimum Length of Lease Required	15 years
9	Usual Length of Loan	5-7 years
10	Investment	Yes
11	Refinance	Yes
12	Owner Occupier	No
13	Residential Investment	No
14	Development Finance	Yes
15	Residential Development	No
16	Hotels and Leisure	Yes
17	Healthcare	No
18	Bridging and/or Mezzanine Finance	No

Remarks

All types of commercial property, including pre-let development situations. Particularly keen on portfolios as well as corporate deals linked to equity issues.

Süddeutsche Bodencredit & Hypothekenbank AG

Ottostraße 21
80333 München
Germany

Tel 00 49 89 51120

Fax 00 49 89 5112 365

Contact

Frau Jacob

Criteria

1	Maximum Loan to Value	80%
2	Benchmark Lending Rate	3 month Libor
3	Margin Spread	1%
4	Fixed	Yes
5	Minimum Loan	£4,000,000
6	Maximum Loan	£20,000,000
7	Arrangement Fee Spread	0.25%-0.5%
8	Minimum Length of Lease Required	Freehold only
9	Usual Length of Loan	10-25 years
10	Investment	Yes
11	Refinance	Yes
12	Owner Occupier	No
13	Residential Investment	No
14	Development Finance	No
15	Residential Development	Yes (see Remarks)
16	Hotels and Leisure	No
17	Healthcare	No
18	Bridging and/or Mezzanine Finance	No

Remarks

Will only lend on properties in London - covenant and income driven. Also considers building projects within the EU.

Sumitomo Bank

Temple Court
11 Queen Victoria Street
London
EC4N 4TA

Tel 020 7786 1165

Fax 020 7236 0049

Contact

Alan Springett
Tel: 020 7786 1164
Kevin Harmer
Tel: 020 7786 1161

Criteria

1	Maximum Loan to Value	75%
2	Benchmark Lending Rate	Cost of funds
3	Margin Spread	Varies
4	Fixed	Yes
5	Minimum Loan	£2,000,000
6	Maximum Loan	None
7	Arrangement Fee Spread	Varies
8	Minimum Length of Lease Required	None
9	Usual Length of Loan	Varies
10	Investment	Yes
11	Refinance	Yes
12	Owner Occupier	No
13	Residential Investment	No
14	Development Finance	Yes, pre-let
15	Residential Development	No
16	Hotels and Leisure	No
17	Healthcare	No
18	Bridging and/or Mezzanine Finance	No

Sun Bank Plc

Bank House
Primett Road
Stevenage
Herts
SG1 3UQ

Tel 01438 744641 Commercial Lending
01438 744671 Residential Investments

Fax 01438 730520

Contact

Mark Hiscox
Paul Clark
John Fisher

Criteria

1	Maximum Loan to Value	75% up to £150,000 70% over £150,000
2	Benchmark Lending Rate	Sun Bank base rate (Libor option over £250,000)
3	Margin Spread	2.5%-3.5%
4	Fixed	Yes
5	Minimum Loan	£50,000
6	Maximum Loan	£1,500,000
7	Arrangement Fee Spread	0.5%-1.5%
8	Minimum Length of Lease Required	Loan term plus 50 years
9	Usual Length of Loan	5-25 years
10	Investment	Yes
11	Refinance	Yes
12	Owner Occupier	Yes
13	Residential Investment	Normally referred to Residential Lending Department
14	Development Finance	No
15	Residential Development	No
16	Hotels and Leisure	Selectively
17	Healthcare	Yes
18	Bridging and/or Mezzanine Finance	No

Sun Life of Canada Group of Companies

SLC Asset Management Ltd
75 King William Street
London
EC4N 7BE

Tel 020 7398 7800

Fax 020 7398 7930

Contact

Helen Cooke

Criteria

1	Maximum Loan to Value	75%
2	Benchmark Lending Rate	Gilts
3	Margin Spread	1.75%-2.5%
4	Fixed	Yes
5	Minimum Loan	£1,000,000
6	Maximum Loan	£5,000,000
7	Arrangement Fee Spread	1%
8	Minimum Length of Lease Required	10 years
9	Usual Length of Loan	10-25 years
10	Investment	Yes
11	Refinance	Yes
12	Owner Occupier	Yes
13	Residential Investment	No
14	Development Finance	Pre-let only
15	Residential Development	No
16	Hotels and Leisure	No
17	Healthcare	Yes
18	Bridging and/or Mezzanine Finance	No

Remarks

Lends on shops, warehouses/factories and offices.

Svenska Handelsbanken

Svenska House
3-5 Newgate Street
London
EC1A 7DA

Tel 020 7329 4467/7457 2872

Fax 020 7329 0036/7329 0654

Contact

Simon Silvester
Claus Carlon

Criteria

1	Maximum Loan to Value	75%
2	Benchmark Lending Rate	Bank base/3 month Libor
3	Margin Spread	1.5%-2.5%
4	Fixed	Yes, 5 years
5	Minimum Loan	£500,000
6	Maximum Loan	£5,000,000
7	Arrangement Fee Spread	0.25%-0.75%
8	Minimum Length of Lease Required	100 years
9	Usual Length of Loan	5-7 years
10	Investment	Yes
11	Refinance	Yes
12	Owner Occupier	Yes
13	Residential Investment	No
14	Development Finance	No
15	Residential Development	No
16	Hotels and Leisure	No
17	Healthcare	No
18	Bridging and/or Mezzanine Finance	No

Remarks

Prefers lending to clients with a Scandinavian connection.

UBS Warburg

100 Liverpool Street
London
EC2M 2RH

Tel 020 7568 7726
020 7567 8000

Fax 020 7568 4800
020 7568 0406

Contact

Annette Alford

Criteria

1	Maximum Loan to Value	80%
2	Benchmark Lending Rate	Libor
3	Margin Spread	Varies
4	Fixed	Sometimes
5	Minimum Loan	£2,000,000
6	Maximum Loan	None
7	Arrangement Fee Spread	Varies
8	Minimum Length of Lease Required	N/A
9	Usual Length of Loan	5 - 15 years
10	Investment	Yes
11	Refinance	Yes
12	Owner Occupier	Yes
13	Residential Investment	No
14	Development Finance	No
15	Residential Development	No
16	Hotels and Leisure	No
17	Healthcare	No
18	Bridging and/or Mezzanine Finance	No

UCB Group Plc

Leo House
Railway Approach
Wallington
Surrey
SM6 0DY

Tel 020 8240 5513

Fax 020 8246 5644

Contact

Natalie Howard
Guy Briaux –
(Nursing homes)
Giovanna Green

Criteria

1	Maximum Loan to Value	85% (up to 100% on nursing homes)
2	Benchmark Lending Rate	Finance house base rate
3	Margin Spread	1.5%-4%
4	Fixed	Yes, 5 years
5	Minimum Loan	£200,000
6	Maximum Loan	£15,000,000
7	Arrangement Fee Spread	1%-2%
8	Minimum Length of Lease Required	60 years
9	Usual Length of Loan	5-25 years
10	Investment	No
11	Refinance	Yes
12	Owner Occupier	Yes
13	Residential Investment	No
14	Development Finance	Yes, pre-let
15	Residential Development	No
16	Hotels and Leisure	No
17	Healthcare	Yes
18	Bridging and/or Mezzanine Finance	No

Remarks

Primarily lending to health care. Investment business, now done through Birmingham Midshires.

Ulster Bank Ltd

47 Donegall Place
Belfast
BT1 5AU

Tel 01232 244744

Fax 01232 898586

Contact

R Hanna

Criteria

1	Maximum Loan to Value	70%
2	Benchmark Lending Rate	Bank base
3	Margin Spread	2%–4%
4	Fixed	Yes
5	Minimum Loan	£25,000
6	Maximum Loan	£2,000,000
7	Arrangement Fee Spread	0.75%–1%
8	Minimum Length of Lease Required	Term of loan plus 40 years
9	Usual Length of Loan	1 month–25 years
10	Investment	Yes
11	Refinance	Yes
12	Owner Occupier	Yes
13	Residential Investment	Yes
14	Development Finance	Yes
15	Residential Development	Yes
16	Hotels and Leisure	Yes
17	Healthcare	No
18	Bridging and/or Mezzanine Finance	No

Remarks

Lends exclusively in Northern Ireland and Irish Republic.

Union Bank of Switzerland

100 Liverpool Street
London
EC2M 2RH

Tel 020 7901 1710

Fax 020 7901 1903

Contact

Paul Rayner
Neil Stocks

Criteria

1	Maximum Loan to Value	70%
2	Benchmark Lending Rate	3 month Libor/ swap rate
3	Margin Spread	0.8%-1.5%
4	Fixed	Yes
5	Minimum Loan	£5,000,000
6	Maximum Loan	£20,000,000
7	Arrangement Fee Spread	0.35%-0.75%
8	Minimum Length of Lease Required	7 years plus length of loan
9	Usual Length of Loan	5-7 years
10	Investment	Yes
11	Refinance	Yes
12	Owner Occupier	Yes
13	Residential Investment	No
14	Development Finance	Subject to pre-let on 90% of space and strong pre-sale possibilities
15	Residential Development	No
16	Hotels and Leisure	Yes
17	Healthcare	No
18	Bridging and/or Mezzanine Finance	Yes

Remarks

Prefers to lend on well-let investment properties - particularly retail, office and distribution property.

United Asset Finance Ltd

2 Stich Lane
Stockport
SK4 2LS

Tel 0161 480 3311

Fax 0161 480 7272

Contact

Lionel Refson
Peter Lucas

Criteria

1	Maximum Loan to Value	75%
2	Benchmark Lending Rate	Finance house base rate
3	Margin Spread	2%–4%
4	Fixed	No
5	Minimum Loan	£200,000
6	Maximum Loan	£1,000,000
7	Arrangement Fee Spread	2%
8	Minimum Length of Lease Required	15 years
9	Usual Length of Loan	5–10 years
10	Investment	Yes
11	Refinance	Yes
12	Owner Occupier	Yes
13	Residential Investment	Yes
14	Development Finance	No
15	Residential Development	No
16	Hotels and Leisure	Yes
17	Healthcare	Yes
18	Bridging and/or Mezzanine Finance	No

Remarks

Specialist non-status lenders on small shop, office and residential investment.

United Bank of Kuwait Plc

7 Baker Street
London
W1M 1AB

Tel 020 7487 6500

Fax 020 7487 6593

Email: alstons@ubk.net

Contact

Stephen Alston
Tel: 020 7487 6933

Criteria

1	Maximum Loan to Value	80%
2	Benchmark Lending Rate	Libor
3	Margin Spread	1.25%-2.50%
4	Fixed	Yes, also capped and drop-locked
5	Minimum Loan	£2,500,000
6	Maximum Loan	£25,000,000
7	Arrangement Fee Spread	0.5%-1.0%
8	Minimum Length of Lease Required	Negotiable
9	Usual Length of Loan	1-2 years
10	Investment	Yes
11	Refinance	Yes
12	Owner Occupier	No
13	Residential Investment	Yes
14	Development Finance	Yes
15	Residential Development	Yes
16	Hotels and Leisure	No
17	Healthcare	No
18	Bridging and/or Mezzanine Finance	Yes

Remarks

Specialists in funding higher risk/higher return transactions, taking property risk where appropriate. Speculative development and partial pre-let deals welcome. Joint ventures are considered.

United Trust Bank Ltd

1 Great Cumberland Place
London
W1H 7AL

Tel 020 7258 0094

Fax 020 7262 4273

Email: (name)@utbank.co.uk

Contact

Mike Campion –
Director
Robin Collier –
Business Development
Manager
Noel Meredith –
Business Development
Manager
Ian Andrews –
Assistant Credit
Manager

Criteria

1	Maximum Loan to Value	90%
2	Benchmark Lending Rate	Base rate
3	Margin Spread	2%-5% (Bridging finance 1%-2% per month)
4	Fixed	No
5	Minimum Loan	£100,000
6	Maximum Loan	£2,500,000
7	Arrangement Fee Spread	1%-2%
8	Minimum Length of Lease Required	Negotiable
9	Usual Length of Loan	1-5 years
10	Investment	Yes
11	Refinance	Yes, if a component in a wider project
12	Owner Occupier	Yes, if a component in a wider project
13	Residential Investment	Yes
14	Development Finance	Yes - commercial development
15	Residential Development	Yes
16	Hotels and Leisure	No
17	Healthcare	Yes
18	Bridging and/or Mezzanine Finance	Yes

Remarks

Whilst the main focus is on development funding and bridging finance (including planning gains), the Bank has developed a niche for shorter term mezzanine/equity finance.

Universal Building Society

Universal House
Kings Manor
Newcastle upon Tyne
NE1 6PA

Tel 0191 232 0973

Fax 0191 269 2167

Contact

Ian Stafford
Fred Pinder

Criteria

1	Maximum Loan to Value	70%
2	Benchmark Lending Rate	Standard variable rate
3	Margin Spread	Variable
4	Fixed	No
5	Minimum Loan	£20,000
6	Maximum Loan	£350,000
7	Arrangement Fee Spread	1% of advance
8	Minimum Length of Lease Required	Freehold only
9	Usual Length of Loan	20 years
10	Investment	Yes
11	Refinance	Yes
12	Owner Occupier	Yes
13	Residential Investment	Yes
14	Development Finance	No
15	Residential Development	Yes
16	Hotels and Leisure	No
17	Healthcare	No
18	Bridging and/or Mezzanine Finance	No

Vernon Building Society

10 St Petersgate
Stockport
Cheshire
SK1 1HF

Tel 0161 429 6262

Fax 0161 429 6996

Contact

R Townsley

Criteria

1	Maximum Loan to Value	85%
2	Benchmark Lending Rate	Standard variable rate
3	Margin Spread	1%-2%
4	Fixed	No
5	Minimum Loan	£15,000
6	Maximum Loan	£750,000
7	Arrangement Fee Spread	1%
8	Minimum Length of Lease Required	N/A
9	Usual Length of Loan	10-20 years
10	Investment	Yes
11	Refinance	Yes
12	Owner Occupier	Yes
13	Residential Investment	Yes
14	Development Finance	Yes, pre-let only
15	Residential Development	No
16	Hotels and Leisure	No
17	Healthcare	No
18	Bridging and/or Mezzanine Finance	No

West Bromwich Building Society

374 High Street
West Bromwich
West Midlands
B70 8LR

Tel 0121 525 7070

Fax 0121 525 0572

Contact

M J Nixon
Tel: 07970 130234
C Barnes
Tel: 07970 130213
J Crittenden
Tel: 07968 513301

Criteria

1	Maximum Loan to Value	75%*
2	Benchmark Lending Rate	Libor/Swap
3	Margin Spread	0.9%-2.5%
4	Fixed	Yes
5	Minimum Loan	£250,000
6	Maximum Loan	£10,000,000
7	Arrangement Fee Spread	0.25%-1%
8	Minimum Length of Lease Required	35 years remaining at end of loan
9	Usual Length of Loan	5-20 years
10	Investment	Yes
11	Refinance	Yes
12	Owner Occupier	Yes
13	Residential Investment	Yes
14	Development Finance	Sometimes
15	Residential Development	Sometimes
16	Hotels and Leisure	No
17	Healthcare	Yes
18	Bridging and/or Mezzanine Finance	No

Remarks

*80% available for 'blue chip' investment deals.

Westdeutsche Immobilien Bank

42 Moorgate
London
EC2R 6EL

Tel 020 7330 0988

Fax 020 7330 0991

Email: klaus.schreiner@westimmobank.com
jane.simpson@westimmobank.com

Contact

Klaus Schreiner,
Head of Branch
Tel: 020 7330 0970
Jane Simpson,
Director
Tel: 020 7330 0972

Criteria

1	Maximum Loan to Value	75%
2	Benchmark Lending Rate	Libor
3	Margin Spread	0.85%-1.5%
4	Fixed	N/A
5	Minimum Loan	£5,000,000
6	Maximum Loan	£40,000,000
7	Arrangement Fee Spread	0.25-0.5%
8	Minimum Length of Lease Required	10 years
9	Usual Length of Loan	7-10 years
10	Investment	Yes
11	Refinance	Yes
12	Owner Occupier	Yes
13	Residential Investment	No
14	Development Finance	Yes
15	Residential Development	No
16	Hotels and Leisure	Yes
17	Healthcare	No
18	Bridging and/or Mezzanine Finance	No

The Westhyp Westfälische Hypothekenbank AG

10–11 Austin Friars
London
EC2N 2HE

Tel 020 7330 9200

Fax 020 7330 9201

Contact

Joachim W Schröder
– General Manager
Tel: 07887 837588
Ray Mowll –
General Manager

Criteria

1	Maximum Loan to Value	90%
2	Benchmark Lending Rate	Libor
3	Margin Spread	0.7%-1.5%
4	Fixed	Yes
5	Minimum Loan	£2,500,000
6	Maximum Loan	None
7	Arrangement Fee Spread	0.1%-1.0%
8	Minimum Length of Lease Required	None
9	Usual Length of Loan	5-30 years
10	Investment	Yes
11	Refinance	Yes
12	Owner Occupier	Only for clients with financial standing
13	Residential Investment	Yes
14	Development Finance	Yes - pre-let possible (not for residential properties)
15	Residential Development	Yes
16	Hotels and Leisure	Yes
17	Healthcare	No
18	Bridging and/or Mezzanine Finance	No

Remarks

Medium- and long-term loans with either fixed or floating interest rates. No speculative development. Tailor-made financing.

Wintrust Securities Ltd

Wintrust House
21 College Hill
London
EC4R 2RP

Tel 020 7236 2360

Fax 020 7236 3842

Contact

Matthew Anderson
Peter Williamson
Nigel Alexander
Jamie Szpiro

Criteria

1	Maximum Loan to Value	90%
2	Benchmark Lending Rate	3 month Libor
3	Margin Spread	2.5%-5%
4	Fixed	No
5	Minimum Loan	£100,000
6	Maximum Loan	£8,750,000
7	Arrangement Fee Spread	1%-2%
8	Minimum Length of Lease Required	Varies
9	Usual Length of Loan	Up to 5 years
10	Investment	Yes
11	Refinance	Yes
12	Owner Occupier	No
13	Residential Investment	Yes
14	Development Finance	Yes
15	Residential Development	Yes
16	Hotels and Leisure	No
17	Healthcare	No
18	Bridging and/or Mezzanine Finance	Yes

Remarks

Particularly interested in residential property occupied by rent-registered tenants or let on assured shorthold tenancies. Also considers residential property – vacant or part vacant – being converted or refurbished for sale into retail market or to be made available for letting. New build developments also considered.

Württemberger Hypo

Postfach 10 54 52
Büchsenstraße 26
70174 Stuttgart
Germany

Tel 00 49 711 20 960 216
00 49 711 2096 422

Fax 00 49 711 2096 419

Contact

Brigith Terry
Manfred Weil

Criteria

1	Maximum Loan to Value	85%
2	Benchmark Lending Rate	Libor
3	Margin Spread	0.75%-1%
4	Fixed	Yes
5	Minimum Loan	£1,000,000
6	Maximum Loan	None
7	Arrangement Fee Spread	0.1%-1%
8	Minimum Length of Lease Required	99 years
9	Usual Length of Loan	5-10 years
10	Investment	Yes
11	Refinance	Yes
12	Owner Occupier	Only for clients with first-class financial standing
13	Residential Investment	No
14	Development Finance	No
15	Residential Development	No
16	Hotels and Leisure	No
17	Healthcare	No
18	Bridging and/or Mezzanine Finance	No

Yorkshire Bank Plc

20 Merrion Way
Leeds
LS2 8NZ

Tel 0113 247 2000

Fax 0113 242 0733

Contact

Commercial Mortgage Manager

Criteria

1	Maximum Loan to Value	75%
2	Benchmark Lending Rate	Bank base
3	Margin Spread	Varies
4	Fixed	Yes
5	Minimum Loan	None
6	Maximum Loan	None
7	Arrangement Fee Spread	1%-2%
8	Minimum Length of Lease Required	Varies
9	Usual Length of Loan	Up to 10 years
10	Investment	Yes
11	Refinance	Yes
12	Owner Occupier	Yes
13	Residential Investment	Yes
14	Development Finance	Yes
15	Residential Development	Yes
16	Hotels and Leisure	Yes
17	Healthcare	Yes
18	Bridging and/or Mezzanine Finance	No